BULLIED TEACHER: BULLIED STUDENT

How to recognize the bullying culture in your school and what to do about it.

LES PARSONS

Pembroke Publishers Limited

For Susan and Lee
who survived more than their share of bullies

© 2005 Pembroke Publishers
538 Hood Road
Markham, Ontario, Canada L3R 3K9
www.pembrokepublishers.com

Distributed in the U.S. by Stenhouse Publishers
480 Congress Street
Portland, ME 04101-3400
www.stenhouse.com

We acknowledge the financial support of the Government of Canada through the Book Publishing Industry Development Program (BPIDP) for our publishing activities. We acknowledge the Government of Ontario through the Ontario Media Development Corporation.

Library and Archives Canada Cataloguing in Publication

Parsons, Les

   Bullied teacher, bullied student : how to recognize the
bullying culture in your school and what to do about it / Les Parsons.
Includes index.

ISBN 1-55138-190-7
   1. Bullying in schools. 2. Bullying in schools—Prevention.
I. Title.

LB3013.3.P37 2005   71.5'8   C2005-903308-8

Editor: Kat Mototsune
Cover Design: John Zehethofer
Typesetting: Jay Tee Graphics Ltd.

Printed and bound in Canada
9 8 7 6 5 4 3 2 1

Contents

Preface

Students aren't the only ones bullying in schools. Teachers, principals, and parents bully too. Together they create a bullying culture, with students occupying the lowest spot in the pecking order. Anti-bullying programs that focus solely on student-on-student bullying are bound to fail. Until all the elements in a school's bullying culture are addressed, the problem of student bullying won't be resolved.

Bullying strikes at the heart of effective learning and teaching — and all schools bully. *Bullied Teacher: Bullied Student* chronicles the bullying crisis in schools from bottom to top, recounting the who, what, where, how, and why of both student and adult bullying and exploring how they're all connected.

School boards, school administrators, teachers, parents, and students all have essential roles to play in the battle to eradicate the invidious bullying that plagues our schools. *Bullied Teacher: Bullied Student* tells educators how to heal a bullying school and how to provide students with the safe and secure learning environment they need and deserve.

Introduction: Who's Bullying Whom?

Educators have been slow to recognize what students have known all along: we're losing the war on school bullying. In spite of widespread concern, the best of intentions, and a host of diverse, well-publicized anti-bullying programs, student bullying remains firmly embedded in our school cultures. Our failure to change what bullying is doing to our schools, however, is forcing us to come to grips with the full extent of school bullying. We're starting to realize that bullying in schools isn't just a childhood disease like chicken pox. Bullying is an adult contagion that erupts most noticeably in our schools among students. But principals also bully; so do teachers; and so do parents. What we're coming to realize is that bullying can be eradicated only if everyone in a school environment — adult as well as student — takes the cure.

The Plague Persists

According to the United Nations Charter of Rights for Children, students have the right to be safe and the right to an education. Governments enact laws and school boards develop policies to ensure these rights. But just because these laws and policies are invoked in extreme situations doesn't mean they're working. When newspapers report a student suicide as result of student bullying, the arrest and prosecution of the bullies should set alarm bells ringing. If anti-bullying policies were being effectively implemented, why did it take a death to trigger them?

According to the American Centers for Disease Control and Prevention, the suicide rate for 10- to 14-year-olds increased 109% between 1980 and 1997. A survey in the *American Journal of Public Health* disclosed that gay high-school students in Massachusetts were four times more likely than heterosexual students to take their own lives. Yet these tragic statistics are merely the most violent tip of the bulk of the day-to-day bullying iceberg that floats invisibly below public perception.

We know that all schools have a problem with student bullies. All schools are plagued with physical assaults, relationship bullying, cyber bullying, severe name-calling, untrue gossip, exclusion, unwanted sexual touching, intimidation, threats, and coercion. The only differences among schools are how widespread and oppressive the behaviors might be and how schools challenge and deal with these behaviors. We know that student bullying occurs most frequently in the schoolyard, on the way to and from school, in school corridors, in classrooms and lunchrooms, and in washrooms. Although bullies are most likely to strike in these locations, no area in or around the school is safe. Wherever students congregate, supervised or not, for any purpose in any school, bullying can occur.

Researchers are compiling a wealth of data to substantiate the mass of anecdotal evidence attesting to the scale of the bullying problem. International studies find that anywhere from a third to three-quarters of children have been involved in bullying situations. Gray's *Guide to Bullying* states that 160,000 students in the U.S. miss school each day due to bullying. A 2001 study of more than 15,000 students from Grades 6 to 10 by the National Institute of Child Health and Human Development found that 16% of U.S. school children said that they had been bullied by other students that term, and that more than 40% of the boys who had bullied carried a weapon in school. In the April 2005 issue of the *Canadian Journal of School Psychology*, two researchers from the University of Calgary, Dr. Tanya Beran and Dr. Leslie Tutty, discovered that half the students in their study had been bullied and that the students in Grades 1 to 3 were bullied as frequently as the students in Grades 4 to 6. New Zealand researchers Lind and Maxwell discovered that 90% of the incidents of emotional abuse and physical violence between children occurred at school. No wonder zero-tolerance policies regarding bullying have spread worldwide.

We also know a lot about the bullying problem itself: bookshelves are lined with comprehensive examinations of bullies, their targets, the role of bystanders, and the complex and disturbing dynamic that links bully, target, and bystander. Researchers frequently discover a correlation between bullying and depression and suicide. In their book, *Bullies, Targets, and Witnesses*, for instance, the Frieds reveal that boys and girls who both bully and are bullied are more liable to suffer depression than other students. Girls who both bully and are bullied and boys who are bullied are more liable to seriously contemplate suicide. We have discovered, as well, why some children are more likely to become bullies than other children, and that bullies are more likely to become enmeshed in violent and criminal behavior as they grow older.

More than thirty years ago, Leonerd Eron led a group of researchers in a comprehensive examination of bullying. The group's longitudinal studies demonstrated that most children identified as bullies in Grade 3 were also identified as bullies by the end of high school. By the age of thirty, one out of four of those bullies had criminal records. The male bullies had greater tendencies to be abusive in their relationships than non-bullies, and the female bullies more abusive to their children. The researchers also discovered a correlation between bullying and a range of social problems, including employment difficulties, alcohol and drug dependency, and divorce. More importantly, their studies indicated that the children of bullies were more likely to become bullies themselves. These findings were replicated in the years that followed.

How important is the home environment in the development of bullying? A long-term Canadian study, The National Longitudinal Survey of Children and Youth, confirmed an essential link. A group of 4100 children and parents were surveyed in 1994–95 when the children were between two and five years old, and again eight years later in 2002–03 when the children were between ten and thirteen years old. Preschoolers who were parented with fewer incidents of hitting, yelling, or threatening at home were, eight years later, found to be less aggressive as preteens and less likely to be involved in fighting and bullying at school. This trend emerged regardless of the child's gender, the family's economic situation, or the area of Canada in which they lived. Additionally, if parents changed their parenting style over those eight years and became either more or less punitive, their children displayed a corresponding change in their behavior, becoming more or less aggressive.

A number of books offer a wide-ranging palette of suggestions for stamping out bullying in schools, from applying strict sanctions to "no blame" mediation. We have profiles to help us identify bullies and targets; we have strategies to effect change in the critical behavior of bystanders. With everything we do know about bullying in schools, one perplexing gap remains: we seem to have trouble accepting and understanding why our progress in the war against bullying seems to be stalled.

Research into the implementation of anti-bullying programs indicates that some schools make dramatic inroads into student bullying behaviors, at least for a short time. In general, however, for all the time, effort, money, and focus placed on eradicating bullying from our schools, the results have been disappointingly meager and difficult to maintain. Overall, the effect of these programs on bullying in most schools is negligible.

In 2005, Dr. David Smith from the University of Ottawa published a paper in the *School Psychology Review* in which he synthesized the existing evaluation research on whole-school anti-bullying programs. He discovered that the majority of programs yield insignificant outcomes on measures of self-reported victimization and bullying, and that only a small number yield positive outcomes. Wendy Craig of Queen's University found that slightly more than half the schools implementing whole-school anti-bullying programs reported positive results, while 15% reported that bullying had *worsened* in spite of the programs. It seems that the culture of bullying in schools is more resistant to change than we would like to believe.

Looking Beyond Student Bullying

When researchers delve into the effectiveness of anti-bullying programs in schools, they refer to staff commitment as one key factor, and the implementation of a whole-school approach as the other. In other words, if all the adults in the building aren't part of the solution, they become part of the problem. Granted, focusing an entire school staff on any program initiative is problematic. But anti-bullying programs contain a unique and critical design flaw: they don't address the nature and extent of adult bullying in schools and the impact these bullies have on student bullying.

All schools bully and all schools possess a bullying culture. Within these cultures, student and adult bullies mix and merge in complex and disturbing patterns. While not exhaustive, the following examples illustrate the entangled nature of these relationships:

- Some students bully other students; some of these student bullies are themselves bullied by other student bullies; some of these student bullies bully teachers.
- Some teachers bully students; some teacher bullies bully other teachers; some teacher bullies bully parents.
- Some office staff bully teachers, students, and parents.
- Some principals bully teachers, office staff, students, and parents.
- Some parents bully teachers, office staff, principals, and their own children.

As these examples demonstrate, student–student bullying can't be resolved in isolation from the other components of a school's bullying culture. Anti-bullying programs can solve the problem of student–student bullying only by simultaneously addressing the full nature, extent, and interrelationship of both student and adult bullying.

What Is Bullying?

What constitutes bullying? Why do people bully? What are the differences between student bullying and adult bullying? These questions are central to the issue of bullying in schools, but the answers aren't as clear-cut as we might like them to be. In the first place, we tend to think of bullying in terms of stereotypes: the big, tough kid in class who has repeated grades several times and who threatens other students with beatings unless they do as he says; the grim-faced teacher who strolls around the class whacking students with a ruler and taping mouths shut with masking tape; the volcano-tempered principal who terrorizes staff and students alike with his deafening tirades and dictatorial style. But bullies aren't often that blatant in their behavior or that easily characterized. Would your own definition of bullying include the following behaviors?

- The popular, personable, high-achieving student who presents to adults as a positive role model and classroom leader but who wields social influence to dominate, control, and selectively exclude peers
- The hard-working teacher who presents to parents as a demanding professional with excellent classroom control and rigorous standards but who regularly reduces students to tears with sarcasm, humiliation, and taunts
- The principal who carefully targets and systematically harasses perceived rivals on staff while presenting to the board superintendent as mild-mannered and obsequious
- The aggressive parents who stifle their child's aggression at home while responding to the child's pent-up release of aggression at school with irate, vicious, public condemnations of the school and staff, and who constantly harass board personnel over each and every perceived slight

Researchers have struggled to develop a definition of bullying that includes all these behaviors and more in one descriptive statement. The struggle is revealed in the diversity of their approaches. Loraleigh Keashly at Wayne State University prefers to define a set of verbal and nonverbal behaviors independent of racial and sexual content and label it "emotional abuse." Some researchers perceive bullying in terms of a continuum of behaviors ranging from the occasional and uncharacteristic to the habitual and ingrained. The position of the behavior on the continuum influences how it is regarded and handled. When discussing student-on-student bullying, they even balk at using the term "bully," for fear of labeling children. They insist on a clear distinction between rejecting a child's actions and rejecting the child. While we certainly need to avoid labeling individuals when confronting and modifying bullying behavior, for purposes of discussion we need to avoid misunderstanding: people who bully are bullies.

In 1991 Peter Randall defined bullying as "the aggressive behavior arising from the deliberate intent to cause physical or psychological distress to others." The national School Safety Center's definition added another wrinkle that a number of researchers insist on: the hurtful or aggressive behavior needs to be intentional and repeated. The keystone of all definitions, however, seems to be the systematic abuse of a power imbalance.

When examining the issue of bullying in schools, an aggregate definition combining essential elements from a number of definitions will serve as a guide:

- Bullying can occur anywhere in a school and can be perpetrated by anyone in that school. Bullies can be students or adults.
- Bullies can operate alone or with accomplices.
- A target may be a single individual or a series of individuals.
- Bullying is a repeated act against an individual or a series of individuals who fear the bully's power. An imbalance of power exists.
- Bullies intentionally mean to harm someone physically, emotionally, or socially.
- Bullies often feel justified in their behavior.
- Bullying is often organized and systematic.
- Bullies rely on bystanders or onlookers either to do nothing to stop the bullying or to actually support the behavior.
- Bullying can occur over a short period of time or go on indefinitely.

Although the basic dynamics of student and adult bullying are the same, an adult's motivations, experiences over time, and fuller appreciation of power and sanction structures create differences in tactics and targets. Adults have a more comprehensive understanding of the power they wield and the control they need to exert over their impulses. In most cases, they eschew physical abuse for a more sophisticated and incisive use of emotional and social intimidation. They also clearly understand where they are in the educational pecking order, recognizing the need to bully "down" but toady "up."

Students are targeted by student bullies for any number of reasons. Simply being a newcomer to a school without immediate friends or alliances might be enough to attract a bully's attention. A perceived slight, a manner of dress or deportment, or even success in school can be reason enough to for one student to bully another. Student bullies also search for vulnerabilities in their targets. Perceptions of social or physical ineptness, physical or psychological disability, sexual orientation, and ethnocultural or socio-economic inequity can be enough to drive a wedge between targeted individuals and their peer groups. At the same time, if a student bully is popular, attractive, personable, and influential, someone with similar qualities could be targeted to eliminate a potential competitor for top spot in a clique. Anyone can bully; anyone can be bullied.

Adults exploit vulnerabilities when targeting students, and also target other adults who appear most vulnerable: anyone new to a school who hasn't had a chance to secure allies; anyone displaying insecurity about their role or abilities; and anyone hesitant about resisting racist, sexist, or homophobic harassment or other forms of domineering behavior. When targeting adults, adult bullies are also likely to target perceived threats to their positions of control and sense of superiority. How many outgoing, charismatic, confident teachers with leadership potential are stunned when targeted by their superiors?

The chapters that follow highlight and examine the various modes of student and adult bullying, and place them in the context of a school's culture and community. The "red flag" that drew attention to the problem of bullying in schools in the first place and the reason that educators and public alike have been galvanized to act is the continuing dilemma of student–student bullying. An investigation into that crisis in chapter 1 will provide the background necessary to fully understand how invasive and destructive bullying can be to an entire school and to the twin goals of nurturing and educating our young people.

1

The Student: Bullied and Bullying

- **Bullies can operate alone or with accomplices.**
- **A target may be a single individual or a series of individuals.**

Many people operate under the mistaken assumption that anti-bullying programs in schools are designed solely to save targets from the attentions of bullies. But these programs are also meant to save student bullies from themselves, to keep them from developing the bigoted personalities and aggression that may lead to personal unhappiness and even criminal behavior. We also want to attend to the corrosive effects of student–student bullying on witnesses to the behavior. Unless they have help understanding and dealing with the sense of impotence they feel in the presence of disabling threat, the nagging guilt and shame that their inaction breeds, and the vicarious thrill some experience as they overtly or covertly support the bully, witnesses to bullying will have difficulty growing into confident, positive, independent, and prosocial individuals.

Bullying also strikes at the heart of education. Learning and positive self-esteem go hand in hand: cognitive and affective behaviors are two sides to the same coin. If students are insecure, fearful, or uncertain, those feelings interfere with their learning.

Bullying Profiles

What kinds of students bully other students? The intense scrutiny afforded bullying over the past decade is filling in a complex, perplexing, and often surprising picture of the student bullying dynamic. Students are compelled to bully for a number of reasons.

Control Disorder

Although most bullying is a learned behavior, some students are born with or develop a behavioral control disorder. These children feel at odds with a hostile world: they are emotional raw nerves, misreading and misunderstanding any kind of interaction with others and unable to control their own often violent impulses. Since they are reacting to perceived threats and provocation, they feel entirely justified in their behavior.

Children suffering from a control disorder will appear tough and hostile. These students frequently disobey rules, initiate aggressive behavior, and even destroy property, alone or as part of a gang. In spite of their obvious and constant inappropriate behavior, they tend to blame others for their actions and display little understanding of or sympathy for other people's rights and feelings. Poor literacy skills compound their sense of alienation from and frustration with the classroom environment. These students fit the model of the stereotypical bully. They empower themselves by rejecting any constraints placed upon them.

Teachers should view the conduct of these students as symptomatic of a disorder rather than as volitional behavior, while not accepting or condoning the negative behavior. Teachers dealing with students suffering control disorders should plan their approaches to classroom management in conjunction with specially trained resource personnel. We do those students an injustice by not recognizing and attending to their involuntary aggression, and fail the remainder of students by not recognizing and attending to the range of other types of bullies in their midst. In schools, unfortunately, we are apt to focus on the student with a control disorder and believe we're dealing with the school's bullying problem.

Learned Bullying

Children can learn to bully in several ways, including being treated with aggression, witnessing acts of aggression, or being rewarded for aggressive behavior. An unsettling correlation exists between inappropriate parenting styles and the development of aggression in children. The use of physical punishment, inconsistent punishment, and overindulgence and permissiveness have all been linked to children's aggressive behavior. Another disturbing aspect of bullying in schools is the fact that there's more of it than there used to be. In addition to studies that have shown increased aggression in children since the 1970s and '80s are several recent studies that indicate that the number of aggressive preschool children is still growing.

This trend may be explained in part by behavioral or learning disorders inadequately treated prior to schooling, but it seems, on the whole, to be tied to parenting styles. Parents who engage in confrontational management, "telling" the child what to do and expecting the child to do it, were also the parents most likely to short circuit the process before children complied. In these cases, the parents' inconsistency itself led to higher levels of aggression. Stress of all kinds in the home, including conflict between parents, the individual temperaments of children, and specific learning disorders and difficulties, exacerbate these inconsistencies.

Bullying for Gain and Control

When most children bully, they have a conscious goal in mind. They deliberately use aggression to get what they want from someone else — lunch money, the answers to a quiz, or just the thrill of dominating. These students engage in voluntary aggression for their own advantage. Since they detect a pattern of aggression in the world around them, they also feel justified in their behavior. Punishment usually reinforces their sense that might is right.

Another type of student bully sees social interaction in terms of establishing and maintaining a hierarchy. They deliberately employ coercion, manipulation, and deception to solidify their dominance in the social pecking order and reinforce their sense of status and self-esteem. These students often present to adults as agreeable, well-meaning, confident, and capable individuals, yet reserve a totally different face for their targets. Their sense of entitlement, elitism, and arrogance make them feel justified in their behavior.

Since bullying depends on an imbalance of power, student bullies are attempting to display their dominance by exerting control. Stereotypes are misleading: power isn't restricted to physical force. A bully could be an admired athlete; a successful academic student; the attractive, articulate, personable class leader; or the unpredictable, aggressive class troublemaker.

- **Bullies often feel justified in their behavior.**
- **Bullying is often organized and systematic.**

Bullies are so egocentric and self-rationalizing that they usually feel provoked into their aggressive behavior and justify their actions by hinging them on insignificant or even invented slights. They understand social dynamics only in the context of competition and dominance. Since they have a reduced empathy for others, they have difficulty putting themselves in someone else's place. They feel powerful and superior to others and self-confident enough to ignore the eventual dislike and isolation they sometimes engender among others.

Target Profiles

Targets for harassment can be chosen for any number of reasons, but some students are more at risk than others. Ethnocultural or religious minorities are always at risk to be bullied. If they have other physical, psychological, socio-economic, or intellectual differences as well, they become even more vulnerable to harassment. In *Bullies, Targets, and Witnesses* the Frieds cite a 1994 study that revealed that students identified as having a learning disability and placed in a special program were two to three times more likely to be bullied than students in regular programs.

Complicating the issue even more, targets or potential targets will sometimes bully others in an attempt to avoid being targeted or ostracized themselves. Students who are homosexual can become rabidly homophobic, an immigrant fluent in English will scorn other immigrants lacking such fluency, or someone inept at sports will mock someone with a stutter. Put-downs, slurs, jibes, and innuendo of all kinds are never purposeless or harmless. Many students are constantly struggling to define and defend their place in the peer-group pecking order.

Some students are bullies in some situations and targets in others. Researchers like Olweus make a distinction between two types of bullies. One type is cool-headed and calculating, choosing targets carefully based on the potential reward. They understand conflict and are not disturbed by it, but will readily disengage if they sense they may lose. The other type is unfortunately labeled the "provocative victim." These students both bully and are bullied. They identify aggression as a way of achieving some sort of reward, but they choose their targets haphazardly, become emotionally entangled in the conflict, and are unable to withdraw before they put themselves at risk. As a result, they frequently find themselves at the mercy of stronger or more adept opponents. Emotionally locked into the struggle, they often see themselves as provoked and victimized when they themselves choose the fight.

Although useful as a way of breaking down bullying stereotypes, these two characterizations do little to prepare teachers for the range of behaviors and motivations they encounter every day in their students. They also play into the hands of people who are predisposed to blame the victim. Gary Ladd, an Illinois psychologist, discovered that student bullies engage in a selection process. At the beginning of the year, 22% of the students in his study reported being bullied. Throughout the year, more than 50% were occasionally bullied. By the end of the year, however, only 8% declared that they were regularly bullied. One of the conclusions is that student bullies search for the best reward-to-effort or risk ratio. They sample the student population for the most significant returns in the form of submission, money, distress, or other recognition of their power, and focus their attention on the most rewarding targets.

- **Bullies rely on bystanders or onlookers either to do nothing to stop the bullying or to actually support the behavior.**
- **Bullying can occur over a short period of time or go on indefinitely.**

Some researchers use findings like these to rationalize "re-educating" potential targets. In their view, students who are frequent targets send out unconscious behavioral signals that attract a bully's attention. They believe that teaching targets to change their behaviors can help remove them from a bully's list of potential targets. While well-meaning, this kind of approach turns a school's value system upside down. Bullies become the arbiters of what's considered normal behavior. Should students have to monitor their manner of speaking, gesturing, or moving to fall below a bully's radar? Should high-achieving students fall silent to evade a bully's wrath, or fashionable students dress down to avoid competing with the Queen Bee? Should sensitive students assume an impassive mask to accommodate a bully's disdain of overt emotional responses? If students have to remodel the physical, emotional, and intellectual behaviors that make up their distinctive personalities and characters to avoid someone else's aggression, then anti-bullying programs are doomed to failure. Our efforts, instead, have to be devoted to curtailing and eliminating the antisocial stance of bullies, and teaching everyone the value of prosocial behavior.

Responses to Student Bullying

Depending on the study, researchers have discovered that teachers actually intervene in bullying situations between 10% and 20% of the time. According to one survey, 25% of students reported that teachers intervened in bullying episodes, but 71% of the teachers indicated that they intervened all the time. The fact that more than 25% of teachers admitted that they *didn't* intervene all the time is a clear signal that something's wrong with how schools are handling student bullying. And the gap in perception between what students are seeing and what teachers think they're doing is particularly worrisome. Perception, in fact, may be a major part of the problem. Teachers have any number of rationalizations to excuse or ignore student–student bullying.

Liking the Bully More than the Target

Adults' attitudes toward student–student bullying may be influenced by the unfortunate characteristics of certain targets. Some targets, for instance, may have annoying or troublesome personality traits or behaviors. They may constantly tattle on others, perceive themselves as unfairly treated, indulge in attention-gaining actions, or react overly emotionally to the slightest provocation. Certainly these kinds of targets require some support and assistance to develop more positive and effective social skills. Their social development, however, has no relevance to the episodes of bullying: no cause-and-effect relationship links one behavior with the other.

Blaming the Victim

Teachers and parents need to reflect on their ingrained beliefs about and attitudes toward student–student bullying. They often effectively blame the victim, criticizing the target's behavior instead of focusing on the bully's aberration. The most common reaction — admonishing targets to "stand up for themselves" in the mistaken belief that fighting back will help them develop strength of character — actually plays right into the bully's hands. To varying degrees, targets already feel insecure and threatened. The added perception that they are somehow at fault for the bully's actions only adds to the erosion of their self-esteem. As one Grade 7 target of relationship bullying explained, "Even though I fought back, I still believed what they were saying."

Believing the Bully

The manner in which a student–student bullying episode is reported is significant. Bullies hold the position of power, and everyone in the peer group knows it. Bullies cultivate allies and cow bystanders. They confidently and persuasively assert that they were "only playing" and that the target took it the wrong way, and witnesses substantiate the bully's version of events. In fact, the target may be so intimidated that he or she may back the bully's fabrications.

Dismissing the Behavior as Gender Based

Some adults tend to discount certain kinds of student–student bullying by ascribing the behaviors to gender acculturation, using value-loaded language to describe events. Boys are merely rough-housing or indulging in a bit of normal, macho, testosterone-fuelled posturing; they can't be faulted if someone "can't take it." A girl, on the other hand, might be viewed not as a target of bullying but as someone who takes her friendships too seriously or reacts too sensitively to the normal ins and outs of relationships. The claim that "boys will be boys and girls will be girls" masks socially unacceptable behavior. Bullying by either gender is unnatural, destructive, and intolerable.

Gender Bullying

The adolescent code of silence is especially strong when boys bully girls. Boys expect social sanction for "teasing," a form of relationship aggression that amounts to sexual harassment. They will throw their arms around a girl's neck, make sexually explicit comments or jokes, use sexual slurs such as "bitch" or "slut," or spread unwarranted and untrue rumors. While girls might grow angry at this kind of hazing from other girls, they are expected to accept this kind of behavior from boys. In one survey, 80% of high-school girls reported they had been harassed in this manner. If girls complain to a teacher, they risk scorn and retribution from both boys and girls in their peer group, with onlookers assuring the teacher that the boys "didn't mean anything."

In an article from the *Journal of School Health*, Anne Bryant revealed that sexual harassment is most frequent from Grade 6 to Grade 9, but is not uncommon by Grade 3. Girls are targeted with a range of harassing behaviors, from offensive and humiliating sexual language to being forced into sexual acts. Boys are usually harassed with sexual notes, pranks like having their pants pulled down, and being called "gay" and "fag." Boys are twice as likely as girls to be targeted with homophobic slurs. To many students, bullying behavior is accepted as an ordinary and intrinsic aspect of school life to be accepted and endured. Bullies, of course, think that targets enjoy the attention.

Perceptions of Bullying

Bullies are careful to shield their behavior from adults; they use threats and intimidation to silence their targets and witnesses to the bullying.

Whatever accounts for the misapprehension of and inaction from teachers when faced with student–student bullying, one thing is evident: until all teachers perceive bullying in the same way, the crisis will endure.

Bullying is endemic, beginning in the first years of school and escalating through a student's academic career. With student bullying so all-pervasive, it's surprising that it can be so difficult to spot. A lot of bullying does go unnoticed. Bullies are careful to shield their behavior from adults; they use threats and intimidation to silence their targets and witnesses to the bullying. When confronted, they often claim they were only "kidding" or "fooling around." They commonly accuse their targets of provoking them.

Although primary students tell on one another all the time, students moving through the junior grades and beyond become more aware of the consequences of reporting. Even when offered protection from retaliation, targets are still reluctant to admit their harassment or name their harassers. Ratting on another student breaks the code of social solidarity students create as a shield against the adult world. Breaking the code risks further and more widespread ostracism, ridicule, and harassment.

Since it's so important that everyone in a school understand the behaviors that constitute student–student bullying, definitions are crucial. If they are too general, students and teachers will be confused when a situation unfolds. If lists of specific behaviors are included, they need to be relatively exhaustive. The lists that follow identify types of student–student bullying behaviors and include specific examples of each type. The examples are illustrative of each type rather than exhaustive:

- *Verbal or written bullying*: name-calling, such as using sexist, racist, or homophobic slurs; taunting about physical appearance, ability, or socio-economic status; abusive or frightening telephone calls; harmful notes, e-mails, or text messages.
- *Physical bullying*: hitting, kicking, pushing, tripping, attacking; throwing objects; unwanted sexual touching; stealing or damaging personal items or property; threatening with a weapon, using a weapon; threatening harm, coercing.
- *Social bullying*: fabricating rumors or gossip; excluding, embarrassing, or making fun of someone; publicly sharing personal information, including posting pictures and text on web sites; using friendship or status to coerce or manipulate behavior.

The Bullying Survey

Since students are the bullying experts in a school, asking them directly about bullying serves a number of functions.

Every approach to anti-bullying recommends establishing a baseline specific to a school. Since students are the bullying experts in a school, asking them directly about bullying serves a number of functions. A survey helps clarify for the students the specific behaviors that constitute bullying. Their answers will quantify the types of bullying being carried on in the school, identify where the bullying happens, and indicate how often each type of behavior occurs. Teachers gain knowledge about the number of student bullies who are aware of or are willing to admit to their behavior, and how many students are involved as witnesses or bystanders. The survey emphasizes that the school knows all about bullying and is serious about eliminating the behavior. Last but not least, the survey provides a snapshot of the state of bullying in a school, a reference point against which to gauge the effectiveness of a approaches to anti-bullying.

The sample survey at the end of this chapter (pages 33 to 37) was developed for Grades 4 to 6. The language can be easily adapted for older students. A similar instrument can be developed for parents, asking them about behavior they've heard about from their own children and their children's friends. And a teachers' survey might focus on what they've witnessed, how often they've intervened, and actions they've taken.

The survey should be completed at the same time each year for greater continuity. Surveying all Grade 4, 5, and 6 students near the end of the first term and the end of the third term allows you to evaluate your current program and adapt and focus your anti-bullying implementation starting in September of the following school year. If time, resources, and teacher commitment are at a premium, you might decide to highlight Grade 4 students one year, follow them into Grade 5 with the survey the following year, and use the resulting data to underscore the reasons for widening the survey to include all students from that point on.

The Bully–Target–Bystander Dynamic

An audience empowers a bully. The overt or tacit approval or passive acceptance displayed by witnesses emboldens a bully and validates the aggression.

One of the long-held myths about student–student bullying maintains that targets and bullies are distinct groups. Researchers have discovered otherwise. In a survey of nearly 2000 Grade 6 students, UCLA psychologist Jaana Juvonen found that 7% were exclusively bullies, 9% were exclusively targets, and 9% were both bullies and targets depending on the circumstances. Teachers have always come across cases that complicate the concept of a bullying dichotomy: the Grade 5 student targeted by peers is spotted in the schoolyard bullying a Grade 3 student; the student bullied at home by older siblings comes to school and bullies others.

We're also learning more about the importance of bystanders to most acts of bullying. An audience empowers a bully. The overt or tacit approval or passive acceptance displayed by witnesses emboldens a bully and validates the aggression. Audiences make the episode public and ensure that word of the outcome spreads: a student bully's power and status are enhanced; a target's perceived lack of power and status are enshrined.

According to Debra Pepler, an authority on bullying from York University's LaMarsh Center, bystanders witness 85% of school-based bullying, and three-quarters of the time they support the bully. In abstract discussions, students will articulate the negative aspects of bullying and the appropriate way to respond; however, when they witness one student bullying another, they often perceive the act in emotional rather than intellectual terms. They seem to feel that targets deserve aggression: if they didn't want to be treated that way, they wouldn't be the way they are. Targets are viewed as weak or deficient, and onlookers want to avoid being associated with them.

The Peaceful Schools Project at The Menninger Clinic in Topeka, Kansas, looked at 10,000 children in an east-coast city and found that 10% to 20% of children from third to ninth grades experienced a vicarious thrill when watching others being bullied. Dr. Stuart Twemlow has assigned roles to bystanders: "bully bystanders" are children who induce other children into acts for which they themselves don't want to be blamed; "victim bystanders" are those too frightened to interfere in the bullying; "avoidant bystanders" are members of staff who deny bullying occurs in their schools; and "ambivalent bystanders" are those uncommitted to a role and most likely to intercede. According to Dr. Twemlow, these roles aren't fixed; children at various times may play a variety of bystander roles.

Although relatively rare, intervention from bystanders does pay off. The authors of *Bullies, Targets, and Witnesses* report that, when bystanders do speak up and object, the intervention stops the bullying in well over half the episodes. A bystander's role seems to be a learned behavior. Just as anti-bullying programs are usually more effective with primary students, so younger students are more apt to intervene in bullying situations than older students, and those who do intervene are more likely to be girls.

If witnesses are reluctant to intervene during a bullying episode, what are the chances that either a bystander or target will tell someone about it? As it turns out, students seldom tell. Studies cite the fact that teachers are so unaware of bullying, or so reluctant to intervene, that students believe that reporting an incident will probably do no good. Various studies report that up to 50% of students feel bullying can't be prevented and have no strategies to deal with it, and that 80% of bullying is never reported. Younger students, especially female students, are more apt to go to a teacher for help, but with the fear of retaliation and a reluctance to get a reputation as a tattletale, most bystanders simply drop the matter.

Targets fear an increase in bullying if they tell, and suffer from a sense that nothing can be done about it anyway. Their shame and guilt at their inability to cope with the bullying make them anxious and unhappy. Targets suffer from the isolation and exclusion that removes them from the company of other children. Not surprisingly, they often feel less capable and less assured than those around them and need constant reaffirmation from adults. They may have difficulty forming interpersonal relationships and may present as academically troubled, regardless of their abilities. Peter Randall indicates they may also have trouble sleeping, exhibit signs of depression, become physically ill, have difficulty focusing on school work, and resist attending school on a regular basis. Targets may begin taking the long way to and from school to avoid their tormentors, or may begin to steal to pay a bully's extortion.

Research indicates that targets are usually unable to remove the stigma of being a target no matter what they do. They may be put down by other students when working in groups, are often picked last when teams are selected, and find that no one wants to work with them. They may be involved in and blamed for fights, but seem too physically slight to defend themselves. The more they're bullied, the more isolated they become, and the more bullies are able to dehumanize them and justify their aggression. As one ten-year-old target explained, "I thought I was the only one who was treated this way."

Finally, although we've known for some time that bullies are at significant risk of developing antisocial or criminal behavior as adolescents and into adulthood, considerable research over the past two decades has uncovered the fact that targets are affected the same way. This is a testament to the destructive and long-lasting effects of bullying on all concerned.

Breaking the Dynamic

Before exhorting students to "do the right thing" and become proactive in bystander situations, teachers should know that adults seldom intervene when adults bully other adults. In *The Bully At Work*, the authors state that only 20% of

Although relatively rare, intervention from bystanders does pay off.

Research indicates that targets are usually unable to remove the stigma of being a target no matter what they do.

co-workers actively support a target in an adult–adult bullying situation, and that half the targets are betrayed by co-workers. Intervening is a high-risk and difficult behavior for anyone, let alone students. Keeping in mind that as students grow older they become less inclined to intervene in bullying situations, it's important to educate students about bullying early in their school careers.

See Curricular Complements on page 30 for possible strategies for breaking the Bully–Target–Bystander dynamic.

Role-playing from the differing perspectives of bully, target, and bystander is a one way to develop understanding and empathy in young people. Educational videos, writing in role, or visual arts are some of the other avenues for students to process the emotional content of anti-bullying programs. Through these experiences, students have the opportunity to explore their feelings about what it's like to be a bystander and to understand why people don't intervene more often. Please see Curricular Complements on page 30 for an elaboration of possible strategies.

Teachers need to stress with students, however, that intervention is not only difficult but also, in some cases, dangerous. Teachers should discuss when and how it's possible to intervene and when it's best to seek out adult assistance. Students need to be warned against physical intervention, and be given opportunities to brainstorm alternative strategies. The more chances students are given to explore the bully–target–bystander dynamic, and the more varied the experiences, the greater the odds an anti-bullying program will have a significant impact. As an aspect of education, anti-bullying is a process, not an event. Developing prosocial behavior takes time, compassion, and patience.

Types of Bullying

Relationship Bullying

The most common form of female bullying is the use of relationships to hurt another female.

A double standard based on gender has always complicated how teachers regard and react to student–student bullying. Culturally, teachers believe that girls tend to behave well and boys are more inclined to misbehave. They still have difficulty believing that females can be physically aggressive. This stereotype creates a subconscious barrier to recognizing the endemic social and emotional bullying that permeates female peer groups. The most common form of female bullying is the use of relationships to hurt another female.

Teachers need to recognize that boys and girls bully equally, but usually differently. Boys, for example, are apt to resort to physical assaults three to four times more than girls. Serious cases of physically bullying by girls, however, are not uncommon; conversely, boys do engage in relationship bullying, especially as they grow older. Boys tend to use relationship aggression outside their circle of friends, while girls tend to use it within. Relationship and physical aggression are often linked; relationship aggression can be a precursor to physical aggression.

Although physical aggression is not uncommon, the customary tools of female aggression are rumor, gossip, scorn, and exclusion, and the aggression is typically directed at targets of their own gender. Boys derive their social power from a number of sources, including physical prowess and courage. With girls, though, popularity is valued over independence and competence — popularity is power. Since friends determine popularity, withdrawal of friendship is equated with alienation. Friendship bonds between and among girls are crucial to their lives; with friendship comes strength and support in the battle to maintain individual self-esteem, and even safety against the threat and the power of the in-crowd. The more friends you have and the more popular you appear, the more attractive you become as a friend to others; the reverse, unfortunately, is also true. From the junior grades onward, cliques rule.

Popularity is most often derived from some interpretation of "the beauty myth," a term popularized by Naomi Wolf in her book of that title. A young female who is acknowledged as more beautiful, more fashionable, more socially knowledgeable and adept, or more skilful at manipulating males is perceived as more popular and more powerful. This type of individual has become known as the Queen Bee, as described in the popular book by Rosalind Wiseman. Being a member of a powerful person's clique, however that power is defined, makes an individual feel accepted and worthwhile; rejection from the group is ostracism and exile.

Relationship bullying can be subtle, vicious, and profoundly destructive to the self-esteem of targeted girls. The pattern of abuse is well documented. A clique forms around an admired, attractive, articulate, and aggressive ringleader. She and her supporters create their own code of dress, deportment, and behavior. At some point, the ringleader feels threatened by someone else, either a person with characteristics similar to her own who could provide competition for her leadership or someone who stands between her and a personal goal. She and her posse conduct a campaign of exclusion, wild fabrications, insults, and rejection to single out their target and crush her self-esteem and potential social status. If she is a member of their group, she is expelled as punishment. Anyone sympathetic to the target's plight is manipulated with the threat of similar treatment.

Research has confirmed that many teachers remain oblivious to this type of bullying. When it's drawn to their attention, they trivialize it. One targeted girl explained, "I spent eight years of my life staring at my shoes and no one intervened." She couldn't understand why no teacher ever noticed.

The signposts in relationship aggression may be subtle or overt. Students are especially vulnerable when they enter a new school or classroom culture. Any situation in which cliques and roles are well defined spells danger for anyone new forced to enter the established pecking order. By the same token, relationships are constantly shifting and changing, and a perceived slight or misunderstanding can instantly ignite a volatile emotional atmosphere. Teachers should be on the alert for abrupt changes in an individual's mood, signs of upset and distress, individuals who are isolated or seem fearful, hostilities among groups of friends, or heightened emotions and angry language. A rumor, for instance, is a serious and sometimes cataclysmic event in someone's life. Teachers not only have to be ready to intervene in such situations but also have to expend much effort in tracking down "who said what to whom and why." Without a teacher's sincere and understanding mediation, this kind of aggression and exclusion will proceed unabated.

Interventions at school work best when the focus is removed from a particular target and placed in a neutral context. The goal is to assist all students to understand why such behavior occurs and how it affects everyone involved. Why does the aggressor feel justified in her behavior? What is prompting her actions? How are those actions affecting the target? What are the various ways in which bystanders react emotionally to the aggression? What motivates their behavior? As students work through the dynamic, they begin to realize that all three roles in this kind of bullying are linked.

Students also need the language to be able to talk about their actions and reactions. We want girls to be assertive, to make their feelings and needs known without hurting others. We want them to avoid being passive, failing to make their

21

feelings and needs known. We want them to understand that at the core of aggressiveness is the desire to fulfill their own needs at the expense of others. Awareness builds understanding: understanding breeds change.

Face-to-face encounters in a conflict-resolution format are effective only when both parties have similar influence and power. Putting a relationship bully face-to-face with her target, especially in the presence of other girls in her clique, will worsen the situation. The bully still possesses the power, and will use the opportunity to trivialize the behaviors, question the target's reactions, or blame the victim. At best, the bully will offer a perfunctory apology and continue the exclusion. The target, of course, will take the remedial episode as further proof that nothing can be done.

Targets of relationship bullying need opportunities to meet with other students who have suffered similar kinds of exclusion. They need to understand that they aren't alone, they need opportunities to work through their feelings with sympathetic peers and an adult guide, and they need to develop strategies for dealing with their situations. In these groups they are able to reflect on, rehearse, and control their actions and reactions.

Cyber Bullying

One of the downsides of the computer age has been the natural fit between the computer and relationship aggression. Cyber bullying encompasses relationship aggression and all manner of electronic threatening, and it's becoming ubiquitous. As use of the Internet has exploded among young people, so has cyber bullying. According to the York Region Parent Health Connection in Ontario, 60% of all students use chat rooms and instant messaging, and one student in four reports receiving bullying messages; 14% of young people have been threatened on the Internet, 16% have admitted to posting bullying messages, and 44% possess an e-mail account without their parents' consent.

The anonymity of e-mail, instant messaging, and chat rooms frees aggressors from normal restraints and puts targets at added risk. Bullies can easily post offensive messages attached to a target's name and photograph. A few keystrokes, and those messages can reappear anywhere. Meanwhile, most students are afraid of reporting this kind of abuse in case their computer time becomes supervised by an adult or curtailed.

Access to accounts is relatively easy. Just as students trade locker combinations with their friends, they trade passwords and screen names. Trust is such an important part of relationships among young people that it's difficult to get students to protect themselves. Mass messaging, cyber stalking, or negative postings about someone on a personal web site can be emotionally devastating. And there's no escape from the abuse. Whatever happens online is carried into the schoolyard, the classroom, and the school computer room. With the proliferation of cell phones added to online access, bullying can now go on 24 hours a day, in person and via a variety of media.

To be effective in routing out and controlling this kind of bullying, teachers must first accept responsibility for supervising and maintaining the well-being of all their students. That responsibility requires them to examine and intervene in the personal lives of their students, and to pursue signs of misbehavior within and without the classroom walls. The day has long passed when it was possible to believe that a school ended at the school's front door.

As use of the Internet has exploded among young people, so has cyber bullying.

Access to accounts is relatively easy. Trust is such an important part of relationships among young people that it's difficult to get students to protect themselves.

22

The first line of defence against cyber bullying is the school's anti-bullying policy

The first line of defence against cyber bullying is the school's anti-bullying policy. The policy must make clear that bullying will not be tolerated in any form, including electronic. Specific violations should be detailed and consequences listed. The policy should also articulate that it's a criminal offence to repeatedly communicate with someone causing them fear for their safety or the safety of others. Students need to agree in writing to abide by the terms and conditions that describe the appropriate use of electronic media; parents need to sign as well, to indicate that they have read the policy and agree to the terms and conditions.

Next comes the hard part. Parents and teachers have to work as a team to supervise students' online behavior at home and at school; they have to act decisively when warranted. An information meeting should be held at the school to give parents and teachers the most up-to-date facts about online and Internet behavior. A summary of what experts have to say on the issue should form part of a school newsletter. Parents should be encouraged to contact the school whenever they have questions or concerns, and the school must immediately contact the home when a student's behavior breaches the policy. Parents need to check e-mail accounts at home to find out who is on their child's personal network. They also need to check their child's cell phone for the nicknames that might supply a clue to online screen names. Stopping the behavior at school merely stops the behavior at school. Unless parents are involved, cyber bullies are free to trot home and turn on the power.

Homophobic Bullying

Homophobic harassment is the most pervasive, insidious, and dangerous form of bullying. According to a Toronto District School Board survey, "gay" is one of the first words learned by ESL students and "fag" is the most common put-down in schools in general. Both homosexual and heterosexual students are potential targets, and bystanders are expected to join in on the harassment. With homophobic bullying, you are either one of "us" or one of "them." Anyone defending a target labeled "gay" is in danger of being labeled the same. In fact, gay and lesbian students will often resort to homophobic bullying to deflect suspicions about their own sexual orientation. In this way, bullies further alienate targets by forestalling a sympathetic backlash from the dominant student culture. Students who might otherwise defend a vulnerable target are thwarted when the derogatory term "fag lover" is thrown into the mix.

A U.S. Department of Justice report disclosed that 97% of students at Lincoln-Sudbury School in Boston, Massachusetts, had heard anti-gay comments from other students, and 53% revealed that they had heard them from *teachers*. A survey on harassment in Toronto, Ontario, schools confirmed that halls and classrooms were the areas in which students faced most of their homophobic torment. A typical secondary-school student, for example, hears anti-gay slurs an average of 25 times a day. Among gay, lesbian, and bisexual youth, 80% reported being verbally abused, 44% had been threatened with violence, 17% had been physically attacked and 6% sexually assaulted. Studies in the U.K. have shown that half of gay and lesbian secondary students had been either physically assaulted or publicly ridiculed by other students or by school *staff*.

Since fewer than 20% of high schools have a non-discrimination policy that includes sexual orientation, and since adults who are proactive in confronting homophobia are subject to whisper campaigns about their own sexual orientation, the reaction of most teachers is predictable. In the midst of the constant barrage of slurs, put-downs, and harassment, only 3% of teachers actively intervene and, when they do, they usually give only a slight reprimand. The effect of typical school environments on gay and lesbian students is also tragically predictable: one in three of them drop out before graduation.

The appalling school environment, of course, reflects the homophobia rampant in the society at large. A 1997 survey in Toronto divulged that 78% of gays and lesbians had been verbally assaulted, 38% chased or followed, and 21% punched, kicked, or beaten. Even the home environment offers little protection: one in four students are so rejected by their families that they are forced to live on the streets. Not surprisingly, gay and lesbian students comprise 30% of all teen suicides: suicide is the leading cause of death for gay and lesbian youth. No one has compiled figures on how many straight students have also been driven to violence, against themselves or others, as a result of homophobic bullying.

As with so many aspects of change in the educational environment, teachers need to start small, think big, and grow with their own convictions. In the recent past and in too many situations even today, teachers are allowed and actually encouraged to perpetuate the myth that the "gay problem" doesn't exist in their schools. Administrators point to policies and complaint processes as proof that schools are safe. The facts say otherwise.

Anti-homophobia education begins in the classroom. If the gay and lesbian reality is ignored in the classroom and in classroom programs, the bigotry that ignorance breeds will continue to stain our schools and empower school bullies. Change will not occur overnight. Teachers encounter and battle racial intolerance and discrimination, for example, each and every day, and will continue to do so into the foreseeable future. That battle is an integral part of a teacher's ongoing responsibilities. The only choice teachers have at this stage is how they want to get started. Since silence equals consent, doing nothing can no longer be an option.

To be fair, many teachers are also uncomfortable *not* dealing with homophobia. Professionals who challenge racism and sexism on a daily basis are uncomfortable when they don't similarly challenge homophobia. They hear terms like "fag," "lezzie," and "queer" in the classroom, halls, school library, and schoolyard — students using this offensive language overtly, not hiding it from teachers as they would racist remarks. The lack of adult reproof and negative consequences make such harassers bold. For these reasons, most teachers would like to change the predominantly homophobic environments in their schools. They're just not sure how to go about it.

Many boards of education have an equity policy that includes sexual orientation; the boards that don't will have an anti-bullying policy. The hurtful language and actions of homophobic bullies will fall under one or both policies. Make two points clear when explaining your proactive stance toward homophobic bullying. First, if any part of an equity or anti-bullying policy is neglected, the whole policy is critically weakened; if some bullying is ignored, all bullying is encouraged. Second, sexual orientation has nothing to do with sex, sexual practices, or sexuality; your goal is to provide a safe and accepting learning environment for all students regardless of their individual differences. Think of homophobic bullying, for instance, in a racial context: if you would intervene in a bullying situation when race was a factor, you must also intervene when sexual orientation is a factor.

If the gay and lesbian reality is ignored in the classroom and in classroom programs, the bigotry that ignorance breeds will continue to stain our schools and empower school bullies.

Sexual orientation has nothing to do with sex, sexual practices, or sexuality; your goal is to provide a safe and accepting learning environment for all students regardless of their individual differences.

Steps in Anti-homophobia Education

1. Start in your own classroom.

Stop all forms of homophobic harassment, including name-calling. Refuse to allow students to trivialize the behavior. Someone who shouts, "He's so gay!" will innocently claim that it just means "happy," but students know the difference. The harassment comes not from the language itself but from the hurtful way it's used.

Each and every incident needs to be addressed and dealt with, especially those in which both perpetrator and target claim that they are just fooling around. The school environment must be made safe for all students. Name the behavior rather than labeling the student: "You've just used a put-down based on sexual orientation; that's a form of bullying and it hurts anyone you use it against and anyone who happens to hear it. We don't bully at this school." Those doing the harassing will receive the message that their behavior is wrong and that they must stop; those being harassed will receive the message that they have done nothing wrong and that they will be supported. Different levels and types of harassment can be handled differently according to the school policy on bullying. With these informal reprimands, however, you're establishing a benchmark for behavior, holding harassers accountable, and widening the impact of the behavior to take the spotlight off the target.

2. Normalize the language.

Model the use of appropriate terms, such as gay, lesbian, bisexual, and same-sex. Current events offer a wealth of opportunities to use this language in context. Students must have alternative language to the street terms they've picked up from the schoolyard. Regrettably, too many students have never heard a teacher say the words "gay" or "lesbian." When you use the language the first time, be prepared to hear an audible gasp or muffled laughter; but remember that the best way for students to learn to use these terms properly is to hear them openly and correctly used in the classroom.

Keep in mind that attitudes toward and acceptance of terminology will be affected by the nature of the community in which you live.

3. Prepare your school "backups."

Talk to administrators and guidance personnel about their customary responses to homophobic harassment: be sure to call it bullying. Talk to other teachers about the kind of support you can expect from administration if parents react negatively to a proactive anti-homophobia stance. Acquaint yourself with the details of the school behavior code. If sexual orientation isn't included in the school's non-discrimination policies and documents, see what you can do to get it included.

4. Include the needs of gay and lesbian students.

Don't exclude the issue when addressing other issues, such as self-esteem, adolescent development, personal relationships, sex education, pluralism and diversity, or conflict resolution.

5. Ensure that resources are available.

Make books and other resources for and about gay and lesbian young people available in the library and guidance department. A number of excellent age-appropriate picture books have been published for younger students, and a wealth of fine novels feature gay and lesbian characters and themes involving sexual orientation and identity. Some of these novels are already in most library collections, even if the teacher-librarian doesn't realize it.

6. Monitor the constant assumption of heterosexuality.

Don't let students believe that the world and everyone in it is heterosexual. Gay, lesbian, and bisexual people are found on every staff, in every classroom, and on every team. Professionals need to actively pursue inclusive language and the development of inclusive attitudes to combat the invisibility of their homosexual students and the erosion of their self-esteem.

Anti-Bullying Strategies

Implementing a school's behavior code and punishing student bullies according to that code will not stop student–student bullying. Any punitive approach simply reinforces a bully's sense of how the world operates: the people who have power use it. A behavior code can be a useful tool when dealing with school bullies, but its usefulness occurs at neither the beginning nor the end of a teacher's or school's approach to bullying. The formal and informal suspensions that comprise the "teeth" of most behavior codes have several effects: they momentarily stop a particular bullying behavior and signal that the school takes the behavior seriously; they label the behavior with a "red flag" indicating to the school staff, resource personnel, and the bully's parents or guardians that the student has a serious antisocial problem that needs to be addressed. They are also a sign of desperation — whatever has been done to control and change the student's behavior up until now has not worked.

A school has only so many choices when responding to a case of student–student bullying. The school can punish; the school can invoke consequences designed to educate rather than punish; the school can initiate a participant-centred process designed to develop understanding and empathy. As with punishment, consequences can range from talk therapy with a school authority figure or psychological personnel, a written apology to the target, or rewards to recognize appropriate behavior. A participant-centred approach attempts to develop awareness in bullies and bystanders about the dynamics of a bullying episode, as they work through how bullying affects targets. If the bully and the bully's peers can appreciate those feelings, they have a harder time dehumanizing and victimizing targets in future.

In the hectic, multi-tasking pace of daily classroom life, making the commitment to track down and equitably resolve the root causes of bullying behavior and the resultant emotional cost of that behavior is daunting. On the other hand, what other choice do teachers have? Bullying strikes at the very values on which the entire curriculum is based, interfering with students' ability and desire to learn. Before they even consider the issue of bullying, teachers need to ask themselves "What do I believe is really important about the way people should interact in my classroom?" The answer to that question determines how a teacher perceives the learning/teaching environment and shapes a teacher's teaching style and approach to discipline.

Although overt acts of bullying may seem to be rare in a classroom, clues abound that bullying is often rampant in the student subculture. Keep in mind

Any punitive approach simply reinforces a bully's sense of how the world operates: the people who have power use it.

The school can punish; the school can invoke consequences designed to educate rather than punish; the school can initiate a participant-centred process designed to develop understanding and empathy.

that students are wise in the ways of schools. For the most part and in most schools, they quickly learn that the kinds of negative language and behaviors that infuse the hallways, schoolyard, and cafeteria need to be moderated inside the adult-controlled, formal atmosphere of the classroom. They know that harsh penalties await participants who fight; that doesn't mean that students aren't being threatened with physical violence, being assaulted out in the schoolyard, or running a gauntlet of violence on the way to or from school. In the same way, relationship bullying, cyber bullying, taunting, or campaigns of exclusion and rumor are carefully hidden within the student subculture. When bullying acts and language remain out of sight for extended periods, teachers can be lulled into a sense of complacency. Out of sight, however, should never be out of mind.

Eventually, incidents will flare up in the classroom and the teacher had better be ready to deal with them. The argument that teachers have no business interfering in students' private lives is as specious as the rationalization that "boys will be boys" or "girls will be girls." The exclusion of a student, the gang taunting and teasing, or the sexist, racist, or homophobic comment should be a teacher's top priorities. When a student is isolated and excluded by peers, seems unhappy, picked on, or emotionally volatile, a teacher has to intervene, not once but over and over. Even when students reject assistance, teachers need to keep sending the message that they are concerned and committed to keeping the student safe. A classroom is a whole world in microcosm and teachers have to decide what kind of world it's going to be.

Students are never blank slates when they come to school. Even with very young students, teachers inherit the values and behaviors set and tolerated in the home. When a young student hits another student, for instance, it's clear what the student did. What's more important is why the aggressive student felt justified in displaying that behavior and how a teacher then deals with it. The problem-solving nature of curbing behavior requires that the teacher dig into the reasons behind the behavior as well as clarifying, communicating, and resolving the feelings of the aggressive child, the target of that aggression, and the witnesses to the act.

As students move through the grades, teachers also inherit the values and behaviors set and tolerated in all previous classrooms, as well as the culture of the school itself and the larger world beyond. Decisions made about any number of issues, from school uniforms to the format of report cards to policies on violence, directly and indirectly influence how teachers behave toward their students, how students see their own status, and how all people in the environment interact and learn. If a teacher takes up the challenge to oppose bullying behavior, that challenge leads directly out into the school at large.

Teachers can empower all students by taking the following steps:

- Stop all forms of harassment, including name-calling. Every incident should be addressed and dealt with — the school environment must be made safe for all students. Those doing the harassing will receive the message that their behavior is wrong and that they must stop; those being harassed will receive the message that they have done nothing wrong and will be supported.
- If your school anti-bullying policy doesn't include a process for participants to develop greater empathy and understanding by deconstructing bullying episodes, create a process for your own classroom. Keep discussions general in nature; never centre out individual targets.

- Become proactive by using a variety of approaches to explore bullying, such as including books with bullying themes in your literature or reading program, role playing, media literacy, and journal writing. For further details, please see Curricular Complements on page 30.
- Talk to administrators and guidance personnel about their probable responses to the kinds of harassment you know will eventually arise. Acquaint yourself with the details of the school behavior code. Talk to other teachers about the kind of support you can expect from the school administration.
- Refuse to allow students to trivialize the behavior. Students using inappropriate language and even those who are the brunt of the language will often claim that it's only a joke, that no offence was meant or taken, or that everybody talks like that. A fight will be characterized as just fooling around. Someone who shouts, "Back off, bitch!" will innocently claim that it's just contemporary slang and not a derogatory term.
- Respect the confidentiality of students who describe how they have been harassed or who request help or support for friends. More severe harassment awaits anyone who blows the whistle on someone in the peer group.
- Remember that discipline is a function of program. The goals of any program should be to raise self-esteem; to involve the students in worthwhile, relevant, interesting, and challenging activities; to foster trust and cooperation; and to eliminate stereotypes.

Classroom Management Strategies

A well-managed classroom is a launching pad for an anti-bullying program.

Anti-bullying and classroom management strategies go hand in hand. A well-managed classroom is a launching pad for an anti-bullying program. The management strategies that guide and benefit students in general in a classroom establish an environment in which bullying clearly falls outside the bounds of expected and acceptable behavior. These classroom management strategies include

- Developing explicit expectations, rules, and boundaries for the whole class in collaboration with the students; ensuring that these are expressed in plain language that everyone understands; posting them in the class; referring to them in the language in which they've been framed when defining unacceptable behavior.
- Insisting that all students meet the expectations and observe the rules and boundaries; being consistent.
- Individualizing the classroom program to match the needs of students with learning disabilities.
- Documenting repeated and significant cases of non-compliance. Some students have difficulty seeing patterns in their behavior and benefit from reviewing their immediate history; parents, guidance counselors, administrators, and other resource personnel will require documentation to understand the parameters of the problem and how to assist with solutions.
- Noticing, mentioning, and praising compliant behavior.
- Ensuring that consequences follow non-compliant behavior. Consequences must suit the behavior and must have the goal of encouraging compliance.
- Establishing an acceptable routine for angry or troubled students to remove themselves from the classroom environment and find immediate assistance or a place to cool off or calm down. Some teachers post a time-

out pass near the classroom door; students are briefed beforehand to use the pass when needed and where to go when leaving the classroom; the classroom teacher must always notify guidance or administration personnel when a student leaves the classroom on time-out to ensure that the student is carefully monitored.

Cooperative Learning Strategies

Cooperative learning is one of the most powerful learning/teaching tools yet devised for classroom use. These talk-based strategies can be employed in any subject area and with any age group; they advance a wide range of intellectual goals and develop the process skills students need to become aware of and be able to counter bias, discrimination, and bigotry of all kinds.

Many people equate cooperative learning techniques either with the formal Jigsaw Strategy developed by psychologist Elliot Aronson in the 1970s or with more current, complete programs for developing social skills, such as Jeanne Gibbs' Tribes program. Cooperative learning is actually a blanket term for a range of small-group discussion approaches. Whenever students are working together in small groups of two, three, or more, they are engaged in cooperative learning. For any of these approaches to be effective, students need to acquire and practise a set of specific skills. As you examine these skills in detail, note how they invest a student with the awareness, knowledge, and ability both to cooperate with others in a fair, reasonable, and equitable manner and to identify and resist anyone attempting to take over or subvert others in a group for their own purposes.

- *Sharing* requires students to learn how to
  - freely offer opinions, feelings, or special knowledge in an effort to further group progress;
  - listen carefully to link what the group knows to what they know;
  - give facts and reasons to support opinions.
- *Replying* requires students to learn how to
  - listen carefully so that they can ask clarifying questions or make clarifying statements;
  - respond freely to other people's questions, interests, problems, and concerns;
  - make sure they share equally in the talking.
- *Leading* requires students to learn how to
  - suggest ideas, other ways to solve problems, or new directions for the group to explore to keep the group headed in the right direction;
  - speak up without cutting someone off or impeding the progress the group is making;
  - offering suggestions without dominating the group.
- *Supporting* requires students to learn how to
  - help another group member have a turn to speak;
  - speak without cutting off another person or too abruptly changing the subject;
  - indicate by gesture, facial expression, or posture that they're interested in what is being said.
- *Evaluating* requires students to learn how to
  - indicate whether or not they agree with ideas and decisions, and express reasons for taking that position;

Cooperative learning is actually a blanket term for a range of small-group discussion approaches.

29

- consider how well the group is working and how they might help the group work even more effectively;
- re-examine their opinions and decisions, and adjust them when someone comes up with better ideas.

Effective collaboration doesn't just happen. Students need instruction in the skills required of a productive group member. They need to become aware of the different roles in a group they will need to fulfill at various times, and to be given opportunities to practise them. For group discussions to be productive, students have to be taught how and when to share, reply, lead, and support during the course of a discussion, as well as how to constantly evaluate the group's progress to determine how best to maintain group integrity and efficiency.

Curricular Complements

Some aspects of curriculum and approaches to instruction are powerful anti- bullying forces in and of themselves.

• Literature
• Media literacy
• Journal writing
• Drama in the classroom

Some aspects of curriculum and approaches to instruction are powerful anti-bullying forces in and of themselves. Cooperative learning strategies can be effectively used across the curriculum to the benefit of any subject area, as well as to enhance and deepen interpersonal understanding. Other techniques can be employed in a similar fashion to complement direct anti-bullying strategies.

Literature

Young people can learn a lot about bullying from literature. A piece of literature has the power to touch young readers emotionally and intellectually, stimulating reflection and encouraging inner change. An author's vision can help them illuminate, reassess, and possibly redirect what they believe, what they value, and how they conduct their lives.

For student bullies who have difficulty feeling empathy, literature is a way of seeing through another's eyes and developing a perspective on their own behavior. Targets realize that they're not alone in how they feel or in how they're being treated. All students learn about the bully–target–bystander dynamic in context, and discover more about the prosocial choices and options open to everyone involved in a bullying relationship.

Whether they want a read-aloud, a small- or large-group novel, or a selection for an individual novel unit, teachers will find available a wide variety of picture books, novels, and poetry selections for all age groups that deal with the theme of bullying.

Media Literacy

When students listen to a song, flip through a magazine or newspaper, watch television, play a video game, or notice a billboard, these events create social and cultural ripples that flow over and affect them day after day. But media experiences possess potential for both insight and distortion. A media experience can negatively reconstruct students' versions of reality, especially as media representations can be accepted too literally. With films, television, DVDs, and print advertising, the image seems so real that students accept the persuasive, attractive, and powerful image as the truth. If that truth is riddled with a variety of negative stereotypes, with an unbalanced or extreme view of relationships or violence, then the image tends to reinforce the students' own negative values.

Some people see that link as a reason for censorship, but they fail to recognize that values run both ways. As when reading print, comprehension occurs in the mind and is directly affected by that individual's experiences and values — two people can witness the same image and come away with two totally different perceptions. Censoring media does nothing to change those perceptions.

The place to initiate change is with an individual's *perception* of an image, not with the image itself. Helping students deconstruct and analyze media experiences fosters awareness and understanding. Recognizing how a media event operates is the first step in breaking its hold on the subconscious. Instead of burying media influences, we need to bring them out into the light of day and allow students to analyze them, to begin a process of uncovering and coming to terms with their operational values. For change to occur, students first need to identify the value system influencing their perceptions. The outside world is not going to go away. By bringing the often negative media events from outside into the school, students can reflect on and start to understand how their values have been formed, and possibly develop the empathy that is so crucial to neutralizing bullying episodes.

Journal Writing

The popularity of journal writing has been a mixed blessing. Confusion over what journals really are, how they should be used and evaluated, and where they fit in an overcrowded curriculum has blunted their use over the years. Journals were first used in English classes; soon learning logs, work diaries, and subject-specific journals spread into all subjects in the curriculum.

As well as serving the planned, teacher-directed applications, journals had another use. When journals first became popular in classrooms, they provided a forum for privileged, non-threatening dialogue with the teacher. Sometimes students wrote to teachers for advice, while at other times they needed only a sympathetic and trusted reader. The journal acted as a safety valve for students, allowing them to tap into powerful feelings and, when they were in the grip of serious and often confusing personal problems, to express those feelings to someone else. At times, students would disclose the problems they were having with bullying; at other times, teachers could discern the situation by reading between the lines.

Journal writing can be a potent tool in the fight against bullying, but a note of caution is in order. At one time, teachers could use their own discretion when deciding what to do about student disclosures. In many jurisdictions, teachers are now legally required to report any suspicion of abuse, harassment, or worrisome behavior. When teachers inform students of these legal obligations, some students become reluctant to write as frankly about their lives as they once did.

If teachers are going to include a private option in their journal writing, basic guidelines need to be observed:

- Students must be reassured that, in spite of existing routines for reading student journal entries, teachers will always read a private entry at any time if the student feels its pressing and important enough to hand it in. Whenever students decide to make such entries they should be clearly marked *Private*.
- Students must be advised that private entries *will* be passed on to school administrators if they reveal situations in which the student or others may come to harm.

In many jurisdictions, teachers are now legally required to report any suspicion of abuse, harassment, or worrisome behavior.

- With writing of a private nature, teachers should respond in the role of trusted adult. In this role, teachers may often walk a tightrope with their comments. They need to advise, but not command; disagree, but not reject; sympathize, but not condone. They should see themselves as adult friends responding to student friends.

Drama in the Classroom

Many people commonly think of drama in terms of performance of a play. Drama as a learning/teaching technique has a totally different purpose and focus. Drama in the classroom is performed spontaneously by students without a script, audience, or rehearsal. The techniques help students explore, make connections among, and learn about the issues, events, and relationships that affect their lives. Through role-playing, for example, they extend their ability to grapple with problems like bullying from a number of different perspectives.

Drama in the classroom can broaden and deepen learning across the curriculum, reinforce anti-bullying empathy, and uniquely illuminate how people make sense of and cope with their world.

Teacher Modeling: Do as I Do

Teachers have all the rights and responsibilities of surrogate parents. They have the right to direct and discipline students, and students must submit to their authority. Teachers also have the responsibility to present themselves as models of the kind of behavior they expect from their students. From their first day in school, students are intent on learning everything they can about their teachers: their personalities, their mannerisms, their habits, their moods, their values. No aspect of their behavior goes unnoticed. Students have to be convinced that the rules of conduct exist for everyone in the classroom, especially the teacher. Aggressive parents model the kind of behavior their children are likely to adopt once they have the opportunity to do so outside the home. Bullying teachers present a negative model that their students will copy once they get out from under their teachers' control.

Regardless of a teacher's democratic intentions, a power imbalance always exists in any classroom: the teacher is the boss. Since this power imbalance exists, students have to be constantly reassured that they are valued as individuals. Begin with language. If teachers use inclusive language, students will pick up the patterns and use it themselves; if teachers are polite and courteous with students, students will respond in kind. On the other hand, when put-downs, sarcasm, and stereotyping come from teachers, students gain licence to indulge in similar behavior. A teacher's long, angry tirade may still a shocked and sullen class for a while, but the needless loss of emotional control legitimizes emotional bullying. Yelling condones yelling; bullying condones bullying. Angry confrontations promote resentment, heighten conflict, and set a pattern of power abuse.

Modeling positive values isn't a panacea; modifying and standardizing student behavior is a complicated process that occurs slowly over time. But if teachers aren't consistent in their modeling, or if they insist that students "do as I say not as I do," student behavior will never change. The onus is on teachers to prove to skeptical students that power and bullying are not synonymous.

If teachers use inclusive language, students will pick up the patterns and use it themselves; if teachers are polite and courteous with students, students will respond in kind.

The Bullying Survey

A. Names are not needed.

We want to stop all bullying in this school. We need your help to find out what kind of bullying is going on this year. You don't need to put your name on this survey. We don't want you to name other people.

B. What is bullying?

Bullying means to hurt someone in some way. Bullying can be done by one person or more than one person. Bullying also means that the same person or persons do the hurting more than once.

   Some bullies hurt other people by doing physical things like hitting, kicking, or throwing things. Some bullies threaten to do things to you unless you give them money or obey them. Some bullies make you feel bad by name-calling, telling lies about you, or trying to get people to not be your friend.

C. Information about you.

Please put a check mark in the correct boxes.

   I am a girl ❏   I am a boy ❏

   I am in Grade 4 ❏   Grade 5 ❏   Grade 6 ❏

D. This section asks about how *you have been bullied*. Please remember that it has to be the same person or persons doing this to you more than once. Please circle the number in each statement that best fits what happened to you this year in school. Here is what the numbers mean:

   1 = never   2 = sometimes   3 = about once a week   4 = more than once a week

This year in school someone bullied me by…

- doing things like hitting, kicking, punching, or throwing things.

   1   2   3   4

- hurting me with a weapon like a stick, ruler, knife, or something else.

   1   2   3   4

- threatening to hurt me.

   1   2   3   4

- saying things about my body or saying sexual things that made me feel uncomfortable, embarrassed, or afraid.

   1   2   3   4

- touching my body or my clothes in an inappropriate way.

   1   2   3   4

- making me give them money or other things.

   1   2   3   4

- making me do what they told me to when I didn't want to.

   1   2   3   4

- saying hurtful things about my skin color, the country I came from, or my religion.

  1   2   3   4

- calling me terrible, hurtful names.

  1   2   3   4

- spreading untrue stories and gossip about me.

  1   2   3   4

- trying to make others not be my friend and leave me out of things.

  1   2   3   4

- passing around a hurtful, untrue note about me.

  1   2   3   4

- sending me a hurtful, untrue e-mail or text message.

  1   2   3   4

- posting a hurtful, untrue message about me in an Internet chat room.

  1   2   3   4

This year I have been bullied in some way this often:

  1   2   3   4

E. This section asks about how *you have bullied* someone else. Please remember that you need to have done this to someone more than once. Your name is not on this paper. Please answer honestly. Circle the number in each statement that best fits your actions this year in school. Here is what the numbers mean:

  1 = never   2 = sometimes   3 = about once a week   4 = more than once a week

This year in school I bullied someone by…

- doing things like hitting, kicking, punching, or throwing things.

  1   2   3   4

- hurting them with a weapon like a stick, ruler, knife, or something else.

  1   2   3   4

- threatening to hurt them.

  1   2   3   4

- saying things about their body or saying sexual things that made them feel uncomfortable, embarrassed, or afraid.

  1   2   3   4

- touching their body or their clothes in an inappropriate way.

  1   2   3   4

- making them give me money or other things.

    1   2   3   4

- making them do what I told them to when they didn't want to.

    1   2   3   4

- saying hurtful things about their skin color, the country they came from, or their religion.

    1   2   3   4

- calling them terrible, hurtful names.

    1   2   3   4

- spreading untrue stories and gossip about them.

    1   2   3   4

- trying to make others not be their friend and leave them out of things.

    1   2   3   4

- passing around a hurtful, untrue note about them.

    1   2   3   4

- sending them a hurtful, untrue e-mail or text message.

    1   2   3   4

- posting a hurtful, untrue message about them in an Internet chat room.

    1   2   3   4

This year I have bullied someone else in some way this often:

    1   2   3   4

F. This section asks whether you have *watched or heard about* someone being bullied. Your name is not on this paper. Please answer honestly. Circle the number in each statement that best fits what you watched or heard about this year in school. Here is what the numbers mean:

    1 = never   2 = sometimes   3 = about once   4 = more than once a week

This year in school I watched or heard about someone being bullied by someone…

- doing things to them like hitting, kicking, punching, or throwing things.

    1   2   3   4

- hurting them with a weapon like a stick, ruler, knife, or something else.

    1   2   3   4

- threatening to hurt them.

    1   2   3   4

- saying things about their body or saying sexual things that made them feel uncomfortable, embarrassed, or afraid.

  1   2   3   4

- touching their body or their clothes in an inappropriate way.

  1   2   3   4

- making them give them money or other things.

  1   2   3   4

- making them do what the person told them to when they didn't want to.

  1   2   3   4

- saying hurtful things about their skin color, the country they came from, or their religion.

  1   2   3   4

- calling them terrible, hurtful names.

  1   2   3   4

- spreading untrue stories and gossip about them.

  1   2   3   4

- trying to make others not be their friend and leave them out of things.

  1   2   3   4

- passing around a hurtful, untrue note about them.

  1   2   3   4

- sending them a hurtful, untrue e-mail or text message.

  1   2   3   4

- posting a hurtful, untrue message about them in an Internet chat room.

  1   2   3   4

This year I have watched or heard about someone being bullied in some way this often:

  1   2   3   4

G. This section asks *where* in the school you have been bullied or *where* you have watched or heard about someone being bullied. Your name is not on this paper. Please answer honestly. Circle the number in each statement that best fits what happened to you this year in school. Here is what the numbers mean:

  1 = never   2 = sometimes   3 = about once   4 = more than once a week

This year in school I was bullied, or watched or heard about someone being bullied…

- in the schoolyard.

  1   2   3   4

- in the hallways.

  1   2   3   4

- in a classroom.

  1   2   3   4

- in the gym.

  1   2   3   4

- in the washroom.

  1   2   3   4

- in the lunchroom.

  1   2   3   4

- on the way to or from school.

  1   2   3   4

- on the school bus.

  1   2   3   4

This is the end of the survey. Thank you for helping us to get rid of bullying in this school.

2

Principals and Teachers: Bullied and Bullying

Principals start out as teachers and are promoted through the ranks. That progression is the source of their greatest strengths and also their greatest weaknesses. As teachers, they learn first-hand the difficulties of presenting a single curriculum to students with a daunting array of emotional, physical, and intellectual needs and abilities. They learn the nature of discipline; how to maintain order in a complex environment; the concerns, problems, and peculiarities of parents; and how to collaborate with colleagues who themselves possess a daunting array of personalities, motivations, talents, and deficiencies. They learn what a school is and how it functions from the inside out.

Principals can legitimately make the claim that "the buck stops here." Principals are responsible for everything that goes on in a school from what, how, and how well teachers teach, to the behavior and deportment of students, to the existence of a broken bottle in the schoolyard or enough toilet paper in the washrooms. They're also supposed to make do with an ever-dwindling budget, to efficiently implement whatever new curricular initiative comes into vogue, to manage and inspire a staff that usually ranges in ability from brilliant to incompetent, to hire the best people they can find from a small pool of applicants of varying degrees of experience and talent, and to keep parents happy and off their superiors' backs. Principals also initiate, implement, supervise, and model anti-bullying policies.

The Role of Teacher

Teachers multitask as a way of life. Besides designing, presenting, and evaluating lessons, they're also constantly striving to keep up with myriad administrative, supervisory, extra-curricular, secretarial, and collaborative duties. Added to those pressures are the continual demands to intercede in student conflicts and to sort out arguments, rumors, upsets, and fights. Teachers deal with disruptive students, students with behavioral and learning difficulties, students who use foul language, cheat, and steal, and students who berate, tease, and harass others.

Teachers are also on the receiving end of verbal abuse, threats, and intimidation from parents who refuse to recognize or believe the attitudes, behavior, or achievement levels of their children. Children themselves try to use their parents as a threat to the teacher, such as the Grade 3 student who grumbled to his teacher, "I thought my mother had already yelled at you about that." At the intermediate and secondary levels, the verbal abuse, threats, and intimidation come directly from the students themselves.

When you factor in large classes, a lack of resources, political interference in the curriculum, teacher bashing in government and the media, and the lack of respect from parents and the community, it's no wonder that teachers often feel frustrated, beleaguered, and overwhelmed. To complicate matters further, teachers are as subject as any other professionals to bad days and occasional lapses in judgment and behavior, especially in their first teaching assignments. At times, they may be curt, rude, unthinking, misguided, overbearing, and even boorish; they may yell and they may even lose their tempers. These behaviors are ill-suited to effective teaching, but in and of themselves do not constitute teacher–student bullying.

Most teachers use their reactions to stress and the authority they possess as entry points into reflecting on and learning more about who they are as individuals. They learn the skills they need to react appropriately to conflict and crisis, to place the needs of students uppermost in their minds, and to ensure that the image they project is consistent with the values they hold and hope to inculcate in their students. They learn that, even if teaching is a demanding and stress-filled occupation, the nature of the job is no excuse for abusing the power they wield over their charges. Teacher bullies, on the other hand, use conflict and stress as rationalizations for their behavior.

What's surprising about adult bullies in schools is that there aren't more of them. The ingredients that enable teacher–student bullying are intrinsic to the environment. The power imbalance is clear: adults direct and students obey. The prime directive for schools is clear: maintain control of the students. The hierarchy of power in schools is clear: teachers have power over the students in their classes; principals have power over all the students and all the adults in the building. From the first day on the job, teachers have the opportunity to bully students. As they proceed up the promotional ladder, they discover that they now have more opportunities to bully with impunity.

The Teacher as Bully

Adult bullies often don't see themselves as who they are. They explain away their aggression as taking decisive action, their abusive language as honesty, their inconsistencies as flexibility, and their rigidity and obsession with trifles as thoroughness. These kinds of bullies rarely admit to errors; mistakes are someone else's fault. They feel self-important, powerful, elite, and entitled. They envy others, believe others envy them, manipulate and exploit others for their own purposes, and lack empathy for their targets. In addition, bullies of all types are frequently egotistical, unpredictable, critical, and short tempered individuals.

But adult bullies are shrewd when choosing their targets. They primarily bully down, occasionally bully sideways, and seldom bully up. Teachers bully their students and selected colleagues and parents, while currying favor with the principal; principals bully whomever they please within the school, while currying favor with their superiors. Since most bullying teachers, principals, and senior managers have not themselves been bullied, they find it hard to credit that student–student bullying is actually a problem in schools, let alone teacher–student bullying.

For an adult bully, children make ideal targets. Bullying students is like shooting fish in a barrel: as a captive audience, students can neither fight nor flee. They are expected to respect and obey their teachers, as they owe their success or failure in school to how those teachers evaluate them. They are quick to accept blame, and their fledgling egos can be deflated and destroyed with a few, well chosen words or gestures.

The ingredients that enable teacher–student bullying are intrinsic to the environment. The power imbalance is clear: adults direct and students obey.

A bullying teacher is one who uses his or her power to punish, manipulate, or disparage a student beyond what would be a reasonable disciplinary action.

39

As teachers, bullies "kiss up and kick down." The teacher known as the scourge of the classroom presents a kinder, gentler, more reasonable face to anyone who might be a potential threat. Children with well-educated, well-connected parents, for example, are usually exempt, as are children with aggressive, bullying parents. Bullying teachers don't want parents regularly complaining to the principal or berating the principal's superiors; it's a simple matter of self-preservation.

As the subject of teacher bullying is relatively new to research, definitions are hard to come by. Dr. Stuart Twemlow has defined a bullying teacher this way:

> one who uses his or her power to punish, manipulate, or disparage a student beyond what would be a reasonable disciplinary procedure.

But manipulation has no part in an open and honest relationship with students, and discipline is no excuse for disparagement. Based on the general definition of bullying from the Introduction (see page 11), a bullying teacher can be described as one who uses the imbalance of power to intentionally harm students physically, emotionally, or socially. Whatever definition you choose to apply, a catalogue of bullying teacher behaviors would certainly include the following:

A catalogue of bullying teacher behaviors would include
- **verbal abuse**
- **physical abuse**
- **psychological abuse**
- **professional abuse**

- verbal abuse through the use of sexist, racist, cultural, socio-economic, ability-related, and homophobic stereotyping and labeling;
- physical abuse: such as shaking, pushing, pinching, pulling the hair or ears, slapping with a ruler, or throwing things;
- psychological abuse: such as yelling, using sarcasm, ripping up work, setting student against student, making threats;
- professional abuse: such as unfair marking; applying penalties selectively; using inappropriate disciplinary methods; inducing failure by setting inappropriate standards; lying to colleagues, parents, superiors about a student's behavior; denying students equal access to lessons, resources, or remediation; intimidating parents who, through language, culture, or socio-economic status, are cut off from a complaint process.

We want to believe that all teachers are selfless, virtuous, talented, compassionate, nurturing professionals. We invest them with an aura of sagacity, maturity, and competence, and are ill-prepared for the methods, destructive character traits, and selfish behaviors of bullies. Teacher bullies not only wreak incalculable harm on the most vulnerable, they also contribute to the creation of an unwholesome learning/teaching environment. They provide negative role models for their students, incite similar behavior by student and peer bullies, create negative attitudes toward school and teachers among all students, bully their peers whenever possible, and interfere with in-class and schoolwide anti-bullying policies, strategies, and problem solving.

"Unbullying" the Teacher

People outside the profession might wonder why principals don't just fire bullying teachers. Leaving aside for the moment that some principals might actually encourage bullying behavior, the fact is that getting rid of a bullying teacher is almost impossible. When teachers are acting as surrogate parents and enforcing discipline, making a case for teacher–student bullying behavior is tricky.

The behavior of some teacher bullies can sometimes be modified. If bullying teachers are unwise enough to bully the wrong students or try to bully up instead of down, they may suffer such a severe penalty that they may be loathe to risk further bullying. On the whole, however, research seems to suggest that adult bullies are usually fully formed and resistant to change. Meanwhile, people inside and outside the profession cling to the belief that teacher bullies will be recognized and weeded out by their superiors. Needless to say, they're incredulous and baffled when they discover that some of these people not only are immune to censure but are actually promoted.

Formal Procedures

Except in cases of moral turpitude or a teacher "cooking" student marks, principals who charge teachers with incompetence have to follow a long, tortuous formal process, as outlined in the collective agreement between the school board and the teachers' union. Typically, the principal informs the teacher that he or she is being documented for poor job performance, identifies specific behaviors that require improvement, and agrees on observable goals to achieve that improvement. The principal then sets up a timetable for classroom inspections to evaluate the teacher's attempts at remediation. The fatal flaw in the process is that, if the teacher can demonstrate improvement in just one of the designated behaviors, the teacher is considered to have made adequate progress. The principal then has to begin all over again to address other behaviors. The process is usually so time-consuming, so prolonged, and so apt to fall short of removing the teacher that principals don't bother initiating it.

What often happens, instead, is that the principal either gives up and hopes that parents don't complain about the bully's behavior, or begins an informal process of close supervision, monitoring the teacher's every move and holding the individual's daily performance up to a constant, critical light. In the latter case, if the teacher doesn't make a grievance against the principal through the teachers' union for harassment, she or he may eventually seek a transfer to another school. Since the principal wants to get rid of the teacher, the principal may even supply the individual with a sterling reference to ease the departure. The problem teacher then moves on to bully another classroom in another school.

Teaching by Example

Mentoring is another option. In mentoring, a skilled, knowledgeable, experienced teacher takes on the responsibility to tutor an inexperienced or struggling teacher. Mentors can supply protégés with strategies for classroom and anger management, help them understand and program for individual differences, and generally encourage prosocial behavior. If the mentor has no supervisory or evaluative authority, teacher protégés are more apt to develop an honest, open, and trusting relationship with their peer tutor.

In order for mentoring to operate effectively, protégés must be able to choose their own mentors, and must be free to disengage from the relationship at any time. When mentoring is implemented systemically, those key conditions are usually ignored; there are only so many exemplary teachers on any particular staff. Protégés are assigned mentors and the relationship is mandatory. Ironically, bullying teachers may be indentured to another bullying teacher. In the case of individuals new to teaching, they may be indoctrinated into using the methods of a bully at the hands of a bully.

Team building can also temper the actions of a bully. When teachers are grouped into grade or divisional teams to plan and work collaboratively, the extreme or antisocial behaviors of one or two individuals can often be muted in the collective voice of the team. When teamed with respected and exceptional teachers, bullies tend to become more circumspect and careful in their behavior. However, it is possible for teams to fall under the thrall of one or two bullies who can effectively silence any attempts at curbing or changing negative behavior.

The Principal as Bully

Teachers want to become principals for an assortment of reasons: some have a personal vision for educating children and want to improve as many lives as they can; others possess exceptional skills in collaboration or business management; most enjoy the challenge of added responsibility; and all appreciate the monetary rewards. They all think their assortment of skills qualifies them to lead others less qualified. But the accreditation courses in leadership and management techniques taken by aspiring principals have little to do with the kinds of principals they become.

Evolution of the Role of Principal

Most teachers teach the way they were taught when they were in school, or in the manner of their first colleagues; most principals manage their schools the way they managed their classrooms, or in the manner of principals whom they admire. That means that a certain number of teachers bring the same bullying mindset and methods to their role as principal that they successfully employed as teachers. These aggressive individuals find the classroom too limiting for their large aspirations. They relish the idea of being at the top of the food chain in a bigger fish pond: they love the power.

As the word suggests, principals were once considered the first among equals. They were the "lead" or expert teachers to whom other teachers came for counsel. If you had a question about methodology or discipline, the principal usually had the answer. As highly skilled and knowledgeable classroom teachers, they led by example and mentored less-experienced teachers. Although they accepted more responsibility for schoolwide matters and received a higher salary than classroom teachers, they still remained members of the teachers' unions.

Until relatively recently, principals also routinely taught at least half the day, a practice that kept them rooted in the realities of classroom life and strengthened their sense of collegiality. Since they thought of themselves as teachers, they naturally evolved collaboration as a leadership style. Although principals were burdened with the contradictory and often difficult task of evaluating a fellow teacher's job performance, this inconsistency eventually disappeared as teacher evaluation focused on individual goal setting, professional growth plans, and a structure for self-evaluation.

In contemporary school boards, this model for principals has become as antiquated as the one-room schoolhouse. As education became more sophisticated and expensive, school boards expanded in size and required a different skill set in their principals. They began to look to the business world for a more efficient model for their schools. They needed accomplished managers who could understand and manipulate the corporate structure of a modern school board, who could handle budgets, fundraising, personnel, and public relations, as well as the legal mine fields of an increasingly litigious society. Principals didn't have to understand curricular initiatives or agree with them. Someone else could always supply the expertise; principals just had to make sure the initiatives were implemented.

Systemwide evaluation pushed principals even further into the business model. The politically driven issue of accountability has forced school boards into an increasing reliance on standardized testing to prove that their schools were operating effectively and to validate the boards' budgets. In many areas, individual schools are named and their standardized test scores listed several times a year. The impact on schools has been predictable: school boards and their schools have turned into competitive, results-based cultures that mirror the competitive private sector. If schools could now be compared, so too could the schools' leadership.

Principals are more than ever before directly accountable to their superiors. Since principals naturally supported their fellow teachers during strike actions, legislation was passed removing them from teachers' unions. When they were forced to resign from their teachers' unions upon promotion, principals realized where their allegiances lay — up the vertical chain of command, not down. Principals who once shielded their teachers from the political demands of supervisory officers started to act as conduits for those same pressures. Since principals are now managers, teachers become employees and subject to the same abuses found in other workplaces.

Building a Power Base

Although many of the strengths accrued from promoting principals through the ranks have been nullified, the liabilities remain. In fact, for the first major step up the promotional ladder to vice-principal, a liability could be turned into an asset: the candidates' teaching records form the core of their reputations, and a teacher's reputation revolves around the issue of control. Teachers who can keep their classes quiet, obedient, and on task are valued by their superiors. The easiest way to achieve this kind of control, of course, is through the imbalance of power intrinsic to teaching.

Teachers have the responsibilities and authority that go with being surrogate parents. At one time, teachers kept a strap in their rooms to administer corporal punishment. Parents no longer have that option, nor do teachers, and nor do principals. But teachers can still use ridicule, intimidation, and fear to maintain control in a classroom. Those who do are rewarded with a word-of-mouth reputation for "being tough but fair," "being strict but gets the job done," "knowing how to make them toe the line."

Ambitious bullies curry favor with anyone who can help them advance up the ladder. They will spearhead any curricular innovation or emphasis that their bosses want to implement; for example, they will knock themselves out coaching sports and convening sporting events if they work for sports-minded superiors. They'll even enthusiastically support whatever anti-bullying measures principals want to highlight. They ingratiate themselves, not only to their own principals but also to other mentors known to have had success helping others up the promotional ladder. They cultivate and use these contacts and supporters to become

Since principals are now managers, teachers become employees and subject to the same abuses found in other workplaces.

Teachers can use ridicule, intimidation, and fear to maintain control in a classroom. Those who do are rewarded with a word-of-mouth reputation for "being tough but fair," "being strict but gets the job done," "knowing how to make them toe the line."

vice-principals, and redouble their successful strategies as they aim for more power.

Gun for Hire: the Vice-principal

Aspiring principals have to clear the first hurdle and become vice-principals. No one wants to be a vice-principal, and no one wants to be a lifetime vice-principal. Vice-principals spend half their time implementing someone else's idea of what everyone should be doing and how they should be doing it, and the other half doing the real dirty work of the front office — discipline. VPs are the "hired guns" of the teaching profession. In schools large enough to warrant one or more VPs, they're the ones responsible for keeping students in check. They handle the conflict situations that classroom teachers can't or don't have time for, from chronic tardiness, to swearing at a teacher, to fighting and bullying.

Many VPs take the time and effort to unwind the labyrinthine cause-and-effect threads that entangle each situation; they handle a rolodex with the polished skill of a successful entrepreneur as they bring to bear whatever experts and resources the board has to offer troubled or injured students; they can be as stern and as exacting or as compassionate and flexible as the situation and the students' needs warrant.

To some vice-principals, the problem is the child, and bullying is the solution.

While effective vice-principals try to solve the child's problems and not the problem of the child, others take the opposite tack. To them, the problem *is* the child, and bullying is the solution. These VPs wield their authority like a club; fear and intimidation are their stock in trade. They yell, scream, hector, humiliate, harass, and punish with impunity. Suspension and fear of suspension keep most students and their parents cowed. If parents have access to power, their children are handled with kid gloves. But in most cases, like the warden of a jail, a VP has a free hand to do whatever is necessary to maintain order.

When student bullies are bullied, of course, a valuable lesson is reinforced for them and for students throughout the school. Might is right: if you have the power, use it. By observing, bully, target, and bystander learn the rules by which the power game is played. Meanwhile, most teachers remain uncomfortably content; they may disapprove of or envy the VP's methods, but they use the threat of being sent to the VP's office to keep their students in line. The principal is content; the school is under control. Most of the parents are content; they want discipline to be strict and they want the students who "do the crime" to "do the time." The parents of bullied students either are too ashamed or don't know what to do about the situation. Finally, the vice-principal is content; he or she has what it takes to run a school. The vice-principal's reputation as a strong administrator is well-established.

Adults Bullying Adults

Adult bullying is far more prevalent and far more serious than most people recognize.

If little has been written about teachers bullying students, even less has been written about adults in schools bullying other adults. Adult bullying is far more prevalent and far more serious than most people recognize. The first book written in North America about adult bullying in the workplace was published in 1998. Since then, research all over the world has uncovered a startling picture. At least one in six workers in the U.S. workplace are bullied, and about 80% of bullies are bosses. According to one study, more than one-third of people in the workplace suffer one to six aggressive acts on a weekly basis.

44

A survey of Australian workers in 2001 ascertained that 33% of those in the legal profession were regularly bullied by their bosses. In the same survey, 22% of government workers claimed that their bosses were bullies. And surveys have discovered that the two workplaces that suffer the most from bullying bosses are healthcare and education. Several studies of nursing report that turnover rates and errors on the job were exacerbated by the verbal abuse nurses suffered from physicians. The July/August 2003 issue of *Orthopaedic Nursing* related that 91% of respondents to their survey reported abusive behavior in the previous month, most of it from physicians.

Multiple studies into an assortment of workplaces have yielded rich and provocative data. Men and women are found to bully equally — small comfort in a profession such as education in which women are routinely promoted to positions of responsibility. The myth in the business world has been that women would bring a kinder, gentler, and more collaborative approach to the challenges of leadership, if only they were given the opportunity. The reality seems to be that the more women gain, the more they lose.

While men and women bully equally, women bullies predominantly target other women, and women are overwhelmingly chosen as targets regardless of who does the bullying. Seemingly, women who gain power are as liable to abuse it as men, but gender discrimination forces them to bully women. In most cases, men's gender alone affords them protection in a male-dominated society. Conversely, in situations in which women bully men, especially in cases of sexual harassment, men are loath to admit to the treatment they have received or to expose their harassers.

Calculating the Cost

School boards have to realize that a bullying culture left unattended in a school will send that school into a downward spiral. A bullying principal breeds bullying among staff; bullying staff members reinforce bullying behavior among students. As the integrity of the learning/teaching environment is eroded, students become more antisocial in their attitudes and behavior, and more dissatisfied with their schooling. Teachers become frustrated by and disenchanted with the attitudes and behavior of their students, their co-workers, and the school environment. As the school's negative reputation grows, effective teachers leave to be replaced by teachers the principal feels he or she can bully or by ineffective teachers who can't find employment elsewhere.

Meanwhile, studies replicated all over the world have demonstrated the link between workplace bullying and depression, disabling stress, plummeting morale, and a range of psychological and physical disorders. U.S psychologist Gary Namie conducted a survey in 2000 that revealed that 41% of adult targets were diagnosed with depression as a product of their harassment, and that 80% reported symptoms, such as severe anxiety, sleeplessness, and loss of concentration, that drastically reduced their effectiveness in the workplace. Canada's Respectful Workplace Project, in a 2002 study, discovered that more than 18% of respondents used sick leave as a response to workplace bullying; an Australian study pegged the number at 34%. In a 1998 survey at the University of North Carolina, Professor Christine Pearson found that targets spent an inordinate amount of time on the job either worrying about past or future conflicts or avoiding the bully; 37% said that their commitment to the job declined. Apply that fig-

Men and women are found to bully equally — small comfort in a profession such as education in which women are routinely promoted to positions of responsibility.

A bullying principal breeds bullying among staff; bullying staff members reinforce bullying behavior among students.

ure to a school or school board and imagine what a similar lack of commitment might mean to children's education.

The autocratic, fear-driven intimidation tactics of a principal and some staff may give the illusion of a school under control, but the learning/teaching environment is poisoned, perhaps irreparably. Teachers may suffer anxiety attacks and feel irritable; they may be tired, unable to concentrate, and subject to mood swings and outbursts of temper. They begin to experience a range of physical symptoms, such as headaches, stomach aches, and rashes. Teacher absenteeism increases.

Many teachers respond to bullying by taking on a mechanical approach to teaching, doing the minimum amount of preparation, and relying on increased busywork. They display passivity during staff meetings, a lack of enthusiasm for extra-curricular events and activities, and a reluctance to volunteer. Teachers view each other's motives with suspicion and most teachers work in isolation. Staff-room malcontents disparage their colleagues, students, and parents with impunity. Teachers display a shortness of temper and impatience with students, other staff, and custodial staff. Anyone who can find a job somewhere else transfers out. The school is dysfunctional, ineffective, and rudderless. Staff and students alike go through the motions and put in their time. And the school leadership blames everyone but themselves.

In the competitive, corporate structure of the modern school board, adult bullies thrive. Leadership is often licence to undermine, frighten, or intimidate others down the command line. While the principal fills the most powerful leadership position in a school, authority is also often spread among several other positions. Vice-principals, department heads, or subject or grade specialists, for instance, also hold the potential for abuse. Behind a smokescreen of striving for excellence and motivating staff, successful bully principals are busy running roughshod over everyone in the school, cultivating their allies, rewarding chosen sycophants, and cataloguing their success stories for their superiors. In the process, potential targets and bystanders try to make the best of a grim situation through desperate rationalizations:

- "He's having a bad day. Steer clear of the office."
- "She's had a number of personality conflicts in her schools."
- "He doesn't suffer fools easily."
- "She's a little rough around the edges, but well-meaning."
- "He's a bit old-fashioned but he gets the job done."
- "Be careful who you complain to; he's got friends in high places."
- "Things could get worse."
- "She's just weeding out the deadwood."

People close to an educational bully *outside* the school, on the other hand, may be seeing an entirely different picture. Bullying hinges on an imbalance of power, and a bully's power in the school derives from the principalship. Outside the school, a bullying principal has to find other ways to exert authority. Depending on the power dynamics, some carry their negative behaviors into their social, personal, and family lives: some don't. The behavior that's accepted or even condoned in the context of a school can be either replicated or repelled outside the school. Ridiculing and humiliating your teachers is one thing; ridiculing and humiliating your golfing buddies is another. A bully's friends might suffer similar treatment, or may not believe the bully is capable of such behavior.

In the competitive, corporate structure of the modern school board, adult bullies thrive. Leadership is often licence to undermine, frighten, or intimidate others down the command line.

Bullying the Best and Brightest

A myth endures that bullying principals, like feeding lions, prey only on the weak and vulnerable. A principal's superiors use this kind of rationalization to excuse the bully's behavior. The targets are getting what they deserve, the argument goes, and the staff will be stronger once these weak links have been forced out of the school and the profession.

Granted, some teachers have a lot to learn about effective teaching. Essential skills, such as effective classroom management, record keeping, or discipline, can be taught; they aren't character-driven. But teachers who need on-the-job training usually can't get it. Principals no longer accept responsibility for being the "teacher of teachers," mentoring programs are usually ill-conceived and fatally flawed, and the most vocal, experienced staff members are just as likely to be among the most ineffective teachers. Decent, hard-working, well-meaning, and caring professionals are being left to the mercy of aggressive, abusive managers because no one is accepting the responsibility of teaching them what they need to know to do the job properly. Ironically, as we've seen, a character-flawed bully who "runs a tight ship" is often targeted for promotion.

But workplace research is also uncovering the fact that bullying bosses regularly target the most competent and confident individuals in an organization. The strongest teachers on staff in a school, not the weakest, can also expect to draw a bullying principal's attention. Consider the following scenarios that demonstrate a few of the reasons why this phenomenon occurs:

- You are well-respected in the school as a knowledgeable, articulate, and effective teacher; other teachers begin to look to you and not the principal or the principal's official designates for advice and validation; you threaten the insecure principal's authority, command structure, and image as the in-house expert; you're labeled "prima donna."
- You are popular and interact well with staff and parents alike; the antisocial, jealous principal imagines that you are amassing power for yourself to undermine his or her position in the school and the community; you're labeled "troublemaker."
- You are independent and a self-starter; the controlling, micro-managing principal's authority stems from those who are dependent and who check all decisions and actions with the principal before proceeding; you're labeled "not a team player."
- You have no interest in currying favor to get ahead; the domineering principal has no hold over you; you're labeled "loose cannon."

Adult bullies often attempt to undermine and subvert the work of the most talented, creative, independent, and self-assured teachers on staff, without regard to how it is affecting the school. While these bullies are most often superiors, they can also be fellow teachers. No matter what their position in a school's hierarchy, these people see life as an endless round of competitions in which only the strongest come out on top. Since they understand relationships as competition, anyone who resists their attempts to dominate only incites them more and leads them to redouble their efforts.

Collaboration is viewed suspiciously as an excuse to share in and diminish the bully's power and control. On the other hand, the less that others need their permission, direction, expertise, or advice, the more that bullies feel control slipping away. To make matters worse, bullies often mask their own insecurities and inade-

Ironically, a character-flawed bully who "runs a tight ship" is often targeted for promotion.

Adult bullies often attempt to undermine and subvert the work of the most talented, creative, independent, and self-assured teachers on staff, without regard to how it is affecting the school.

quacies by inventing similar flaws in others and attacking them on that basis. Through a constant campaign of one-upmanship, they automatically elevate themselves and subdue their own self-doubts. In whatever way they can, bullies slowly chip away at the core of self-actualization that motivates highly proficient people.

Sexual Harassment

The gender-based power imbalance among co-workers adds another layer of complexity to adult–adult bullying in any workplace, and especially in a school. When you mix power, sexuality, and gender you have the recipe for sexual harassment. As with other forms of bullying, sexual harassment is rooted in power abuse rather than sexuality, and represents another avenue for bullies to dominate others and assert superiority.

The research into workplace bullying of a sexual nature indicates that it's pervasive. Among co-workers in a traditional, male-dominated society, men are more likely to sexualize the workplace. If their upbringing has supported the concept of women being subservient to men, they will more than likely bring those attitudes to where they work. These men will present no differently than other men: they may be personable, efficient, hard-working, and honest. They may also be sexual harassers. If, however, men and women are equally represented in the workplace, the power balance reaches equilibrium and problems with sexual harassment are reduced.

Just because the behavior isn't reported doesn't mean it's not there. Consider the situation in many elementary schools in which women form the overwhelming majority among staff members. If the principal is also a woman and a bully, the female bullies on staff may feel licensed to sexually harass male staff members. Often relatively inexperienced teachers, these men may find themselves the butt of sexual jokes and innuendo, and suffer a constant barrage of inappropriate remarks and behavior. Statistically, few men report sexual harassment. In a male-dominated society, most men may fear being ridiculed for disliking, suffering from, and resisting a woman's inappropriate behavior.

Most boards have anti-sexual harassment policies and reporting procedures. The presence of a policy satisfies their responsibility under law to have protective measures in place; they can't be sued for negligence on that basis. The policy gives an individual the right to complain but does nothing to stop the behavior.

When the principal is the offender or condones the behavior, or when a powerful faction of a staff approves the behavior, it's difficult for an individual to stand up against the abuse. If the target is a probationary teacher, an experienced teacher due to be evaluated by a bullying principal or vice-principal, or any member of staff insecure about his or her abilities or proficiencies, the power imbalance behind the abuse can be overwhelming. For gay and lesbian teachers, depending on where they work, outing themselves in the process of revealing sexual harassment can end their careers.

Identifying the Bully

With student bullying, the first priority is to stop the behavior. The process that follows that initial action is designed to address the harm done to the target, initiate change in the bully, and educate bystanders to their role in the behavior and their responsibilities to all concerned, including themselves. With adult bullying, the first priority is still to stop the behavior. If the bully is a teacher, that responsibility falls first to the principal and then to the teacher's colleagues; inaction by either equals consent to and complicity in the bullying behavior. If the principal is a bully, the task of stopping the behavior takes on herculean proportions.

Many people naively believe that all they have to do is bring the principal's offensive behavior to the principal's attention and allow self-awareness to dawn, and contrition and change will soon follow. If bosses bullying in the workplace are any indication, that's not what usually happens. A bully's behavior is rooted in personal values that have become ingrained over time. The behavior is consistent with how they understand the world to operate. Since the behavior has served them well and has successfully placed them in a position of authority over others, bullying bosses see a logical cause-and-effect relationship between their behavior and their success. Their sense of superiority and possible lack of empathy invest them with an almost impenetrable shield of arrogance that makes any attempt to make them "see through the eyes of another" virtually impossible. Without self-recognition, behavior will not change.

When bullied, adult targets tend to question themselves and their own abilities. They soul search and agonize over every detail of what they've said, how they've said it, or what they've done or not done to incur the bully's displeasure. The hunt for a cause needs to extend outward, however, not inward. The bully's action and reactions have to be recognized for what they are: aggression.

Adult bullies, on the other hand, need to recognize the conflict around them and begin to look inward for the causes. Most of the following behaviors will emanate from a superior — a principal, vice-principal, or department head — and some might come from a tenured, more experienced, or more senior colleague. They all constitute bullying and all are untenable. The lists are not exhaustive.

You'll know you're in the presence of a bully, if the individual

- routinely uses offensive and suggestive language, and makes derogatory or degrading remarks;
- indulges in unwelcome and coercive sexual behavior, including making unwanted physical or sexually harassing contact, or displaying suggestive or sexist material;
- makes racist, sexist, or homophobic jokes or comments;
- often utters embarrassing, threatening, humiliating, patronizing, or intimidating remarks;
- indulges in reprisals, spreads false rumors, or attempts to socially isolate and ostracize another.

You'll know *you're* being bullied if your superior or colleague

- makes you the target of any of the behaviors from the list above;
- constantly insults you and puts you down; makes rude, degrading, or insulting remarks;
- yells or screams at you or gives vent to emotional outbursts directed at you; moves overly closely when speaking to you; finger points, pounds the desk, tears up paper angrily;
- constantly interrupts you and keeps you from expressing yourself;
- constantly makes fun of your convictions, tastes, or political choices; makes you the target of jokes;

- unfairly questions or criticizes your abilities;
- holds you to standards and expectations different from or more rigorous than those of your colleagues;
- blames you when unreasonable parents unfairly criticize your program, your teaching, or how you deal with their child; refuses to discipline students from your classroom;
- withholds resources given to other teachers (e.g., new texts, opportunities for in-servicing, money for special classroom programs, reimbursement for out-of-pocket expenses for supplies not available in the school);
- threatens a letter of censure in your personnel file or other disciplinary measures for minor infractions;
- censures you for occasional, inadvertent, or unavoidable oversights, such as being late for yard duty or not handing a report in on time, but overlooks similar infractions in others;
- threatens you unfairly with a poor performance evaluation;
- discounts or ignores your positive contributions;
- takes credit for your work, such as organizing extra-curricular events or fundraising;
- criticizes or belittles you in front of students or other staff members,

Blaming the Victim

Be wary if your principal utters the phrase, "personality conflict." It doesn't mean that you agree to disagree. Inherent in the language is the assumption that the principal has been driven to lapses in judgment by the behavior of the target.

Be careful, as well, to distinguish between positive and negative criticism. The relentless plan–teach–test–mark cycle leaves every teacher vulnerable to criticism. The work is never finished and the job never ends. A negative, nit-picking superior can find fault with anyone at any time, and anyone's self-confidence can be undermined when constantly being criticized. Your stress and anxiety levels will be constantly elevated and you'll eventually begin to doubt yourself. You'll find yourself second-guessing everything you do or say, and reexamining your every action and word. You'll progress from defensively asking yourself "Am I leaving myself open to criticism if I do this?" to wondering "Am I doing the right thing?" Soon you'll be so tied up in knots you'll be reluctant to make the smallest decision on your own. You've been belittled, diminished, and neutralized by a bully.

Deconstructing Bullying Behavior

Sometimes bullying principals display such a disconcertingly inconsistent and erratic pattern of abuse that it's hard to credit or understand what's going on. They might have a positive, intellectual sense of what they want to accomplish in a school, for example, and be able to articulate a plan of action, but they are so emotionally dysfunctional that putting those plans into practice creates an intolerable level of stress. The more they try to do, the more they come face to face with their own insecurities or inadequacies. When they have difficulty coping, they can't restrain their emotions. But those emotions are released selectively.

These kinds of bullies always weigh the risk/reward ratio before giving full rein to their feelings. They could be talking to a parent or a superior on the telephone in a most reasonable and professional manner, and then explode, spontaneously

Be wary if your principal utters the phrase, "personality conflict."

The behavior and manner of bully principals can be contradictory and confusing. They see themselves as misunderstood and put upon when, in fact, they are destructive and dysfunctional.

and at random, at anyone in their path. They may claim that they're having a bad day, and use that as an excuse to shut down any and all who need their support or action. Some will conduct a public tirade in the office or in a staff meeting, informing one and all in an angry, ear-piercing tone how busy they are and that teachers are supposed to solve their own problems. The volatile outburst serves as an invisible shield, warding off any new business except for the direst of emergencies.

These bully principals seldom target a single individual over a period of time, unless that person has caused them to lose face with school staff, their superiors, or the community. Although anyone in their path can turn into a target, they're still careful about whom they bully. When their stress levels rise, they give vent to their aggressive emotions only when they feel they have nothing to lose and won't be held accountable for their actions. They seldom acknowledge or apologize for their abusive tone or behavior because that would be an admission of a loss of control. A sense of control is the key to the behavior. Rigid and obsessive, the more these people feel themselves unable to control their environment, the more stress they feel, and the greater the need to relieve that stress at someone else's expense.

The behavior and manner of bully principals can be contradictory and confusing. Everyone around them is usually on tenterhooks, never knowing from one moment to the next what will set them off or whom they will target next. Meanwhile, bully principals never truly understand the impact they have or why they encounter so much friction and interpersonal discord in their schools. They see themselves as misunderstood and put upon when, in fact, they are destructive and dysfunctional.

Bullying Bosses and the Law

Some acts of aggression may fit the definition of adult–adult bullying but are so severe that they move beyond the bounds of antisocial behavior into the realm of law breaking. Physical assault, assault with a weapon, threats to hurt or kill, sexual abuse, and theft are examples of criminal behavior that warrants police intervention. Most adult bullies in schools are careful to stay on the legal side of bullying, but the regulations that govern bullying aren't always clear on where the line is drawn between dislikable bosses and bosses who mean to do harm. Being ill-tempered, manipulative, dishonest, rude, inconsistent, unsupportive, boorish, and generally obnoxious makes someone ill-suited to be a teacher, a vice-principal, or a principal. But that behavior is not against the law.

If a bullying principal targets you in your school, the existence of a law or policy gives you the right to sue or seek redress: it doesn't necessarily solve your problem. Research into workplace bullying has discovered that a bullying boss's superiors usually will do nothing to support the employee target or will support the bully. When the burden of proof is on you, and the board's resources are directed toward supporting principals, you have an uphill battle.

Some cases are easier to prove than others. If you can prove that the abuse you suffered is because of your status as a member of a protected group — as defined by characteristics such as gender, nationality, race, religion, age, disability, and, in some jurisdictions, sexual orientation — you can probably make a human rights claim against the bully and make it stick. The process is complicated, convoluted, and time-consuming; the action taken against the bully, if he or she is proven culpable, usually amounts to a slap on the wrist. Most school boards have anti-discrimination policies that mirror human rights policies, and union representatives can guide teachers through the appropriate procedures to lodge a complaint or grievance. This process is also complicated, convoluted, and time-consuming; the action taken against the bully, if he or she is proven culpable, also usually amounts to a slap on the wrist.

Keep in mind, as well, that if you are a member of a group with protected status and your principal is a member of that same group, discrimination will be hard to prove. In the United States, as of this writing, workplace abuse can be deemed discriminatory and illegal only if the target is a member of a protected status group and the bully is *not* a member of that group. A racial slur from one person of color to another, for example, would be inexcusable and unacceptable — but not illegal.

On the other hand, you don't have to be a member of a protected group to charge someone with an offence if, for instance, the person displays sexist, racist, or homophobic behavior in a way that "poisons" the work environment. In a school environment, the adult bully's behavior can be traced down the line to harm done to children. Regardless of how difficult it might be, that behavior has to be stopped.

Reacting to Bullying

When a boss bullies in the workplace, support for a target is hard to come by.

If a principal is bullying you, the first hurdle to overcome is your own rationalization and self-delusion. Most people want to avoid conflict and stay out of trouble, and hope for the best. When they recognize they're being bullied, especially by the principal, they react initially in such self-defeating ways as the following:

- I love teaching. I'll just try to avoid the principal as much as I can and get my satisfaction from the classroom.
- The principal is probably going through a difficult time right now; things will get better when he gets through this rough spot.
- I could transfer schools but I could just as easily run into someone worse; "better the devil you know."
- I'll just wait the principal out; she has only a few more years in this school; when she goes things will be better.
- I'll just have to learn how not to provoke him.
- If I stand up to her, things will only get worse.
- It doesn't matter how I'm being treated; I get paid no matter what happens.

Once the pattern of abuse becomes insufferable and the target finally realizes that something must be done about the principal's behavior, the target naively assumes that other people in the school and the board will rally around and see justice done. Unfortunately, that's usually *not* what happens.

When a boss bullies in the workplace, support for a target is hard to come by. There is no guarantee you will get a sympathetic hearing from someone up the line — a vice-principal, principal, or superintendent of schools. According to one study, the bully's immediate superior either aided the bully or punished the target in nearly half the cases investigated. Additionally, superiors, human resources personnel, and co-workers took positive action in support of the target less than

The same teachers who harangue student bystanders about their passive response to episodes of bullying usually do nothing to intervene or help a colleague who has been targeted.

20% if the time. About half of the co-workers actually betrayed the target. Positive support for targets came only from family and friends outside the workplace.

The response of co-workers is especially relevant in an educational setting. Much has been written about the behavior of student witnesses to bullying and how they have to learn how and when to intercede. The same teachers who harangue student bystanders about their passive response to episodes of bullying usually do nothing to intervene or help a colleague who has been targeted. Their reasons for inaction are similar to those for their students' lack of response. Some have a foxhole mentality about a target's trauma: they're glad it's not them and they're ashamed of feeling that way. They're afraid to take the target's side in case the bully turns on them. There's also a tendency to blame the victim: the target must be incompetent or in some way at fault for the attack. Adult bullies often encourage this assumption. They divide and conquer. By praising and gifting the target's colleagues most likely to intervene, the bully enlists them as unwitting allies.

The standard advice we give students who are bullied is tell an adult. If you're an adult, whom do you tell? Since bullies hector down the ladder and not up, you will probably have difficulty convincing a principal's superiors that the self-effacing, personable, and accommodating individual they know is driving you to depression. Most bullies are also selective. A few will terrorize everyone in the building, including office staff, teachers, and students. Usually, however, a bully will show one face to one person and a different face to someone else. They may even be charming to a teacher and, without warning, turn on that same person. Some principals are serial bullies, attacking one target for a period of time before moving on to another. Uncertainty and inconsistency are their stock in trade.

Fighting Back

Dealing with an adult bully is hard; dealing with someone in a powerful position, such as a principal, is harder still. If you hope to be successful, you have to neutralize the bully's power imbalance through a meticulous, step-by-step campaign.

1. Talk to Someone

When you suspect that you're being bullied, your immediate reaction is to turn inward, questioning yourself and your abilities. The longer you remain isolated in this reflective state, the less objective you become. You must shut down the introspection and regain your perspective and objectivity. You can accomplish this goal only by reaching out to others. Once you entertain the possibility that you're being bullied, you have to find someone to talk to about it. Other people provide validation, reassurance, strength, and credibility.

First, approach someone outside the school, a family member or friend whose opinion you value, and tell them what's been happening to you. Simply venting, while necessary at the beginning, is no solution. You need to create a problem-solving dialogue, not a daily whine. Your friends and family will be sympathetic for a time, but you can quickly burn them out. You may want to investigate and consider employee assistance programs, but only if strict confidentiality is assured and a neutral site is available.

You have to neutralize the bully's power step by step:

1. Talk to someone
2. Accept that you're a target
3. Document
4. Enlist allies
5. Call your union or federation
6. Name the behavior
7. Confront the bully

2. Accept that You're a Target

Acknowledge what is happening to you and that you are not to blame. Recognize that you are responsible only for your own behavior and not your principal's. Realize that your only choices are to fight or flee. Clinging to the hope that the bully will change is folly.

3. Document

Write down the details of any and all conflicts with the principal, including language, tone of voice, and body language. Describe what happened and when; record the presence of witnesses, if any, and your own reactions to what happened. Describe how the abuse affects you personally, your approach to tasks, your attitude toward school, and your dealings with staff and students. Developing documentation is time-consuming, laborious, and crucial; one of the ways you can counter a principal's power and a board's skepticism is through objective evidence. Arm yourself with the facts.

4. Enlist Allies

Carefully sound out your friends on staff or others who may have suffered abuse similar to yours. "Carefully" is the operative word. Bullying principals often build a foundation of trust and sympathy among selective staff members from which to launch their attacks against others on staff. When you talk to your colleagues, find out what their feelings are about the principal. Discover if they've had similar experiences to yours and, if so, what they did about it. Ask if they would be supportive if you approached the principal. Find out if anyone else on staff will join you in standing up to the bully.

5. Call Your Union or Federation

Dealing with a bullying principal or colleague may be new to you, but it is not to your union or federation. Discuss your options with a union representative from outside the school. Present your documentation and whatever you've discovered about the principal's schoolwide pattern of abuse. Try to discover if the bully has a history of abusive behavior. Arrange for someone to attend meetings with you and the principal if you decide to go that route.

6. Name the Behavior

You haven't as yet decided whether you'll remain in the school or transfer out as soon as you can. What you have decided is that you will no longer be bullied and that you will never sink to the bully's tactics.

"Naming the behavior" is a basic self-defence technique. In any conflict situation, the use of pejorative terms such as "bully" usually ignites an exchange of name-calling and denials, and escalates the conflict. If a teacher being harangued by a principal says, "Everyone knows you're a bully but you're not going to intimidate me," the principal would probably feel unfairly attacked and reply in kind. Instead, avoid using labels or sarcasm, or making assumptions about the principal's motives. Speak directly to the person and the specific behavior.

Naming the behavior requires a plain declaration of fact and an expression of the target's resultant feelings. If teacher is being harangued, the teacher would declare, "I'm feeling uneasy and threatened right now because you've been presenting your own case in a loud voice and I haven't had a chance to speak." If the principal invades the teacher's personal space in an intimidating manner, the teacher would say, "You're crowding me and I feel uncomfortable; please move back." If the principal kept interrupting, the teacher would explain, "You're interrupting me before I finish. Please let me finish and I won't interrupt you when you reply. Then maybe we can understand each other better." Whenever possible, ask for feedback, such as "How do you feel about that?" The bullying principal would be hard-pressed to deny the facts or the expressed feelings and, chances are, would become more circumspect and less overtly confrontational.

7. *Confront the Bully*

- **Make sure the initial confrontation occurs in private.**
- **Name the behavior but don't label it.**
- **Don't try to analyze the bully's behavior.**
- **Keep records.**

Nurses have invented a response to bullying incidents — the Code Pink. When a known bullying physician blows up at a nurse, a Code Pink alert is spread; all available nurses rush to the scene and silently stand by the target in support. Unfortunately, such a strategy doesn't work in a school situation. With all teachers locked in separate classrooms, few would be able to respond even if such a code could be spread. When you first confront the bully, it will probably be by yourself.

Confrontation probably won't stop the bully from harassing other people, but it may stop the bully from harassing you. Make sure the initial confrontation occurs in private, such as in the bully's office or classroom, and that there is no audience. Without the presence of supporters or the face-saving behavior prompted by an audience, the bully is more apt to either back down or be more reasonable. Name the behavior but don't label it. You don't want to get into an argument about what is or is not bullying, the bully's intentions, or any number of diversionary and specious tangents. Declare the behavior unjustified and unacceptable, and state that you intend to put a stop to it. The bully may become confused, disempowered, and neutralized when someone else sets limits on what they do. Bullies can't control their own antisocial behavior, but they can accept limits to that behavior.

It's helpful if you know about others who receive the same kind of harassment as you, and if you can describe a pattern of abuse and the effect it's had. Bullying principals are often unaware of how widespread, frequent, public, and harmful their behavior is. The more they understand that their behavior is noticed and can be articulated, the more they have to fear from accountability. They also think that people admire them for their strength, assertiveness, and decisiveness. Give them a view of their true reputation. At the same time, give them credit when it's deserved and allow them to save face. Cite times when they supported you or demonstrated positive leadership in the school. Make it clear that you aren't rejecting them, just their behavior.

Don't try to analyze the bully's behavior. The long chain of conscious and unconscious events that has resulted in your being bullied defies simple analysis. Don't worry about the bully's motivations. Your goal is to stop the behavior, not understand it. If you're yelled at, walk away and document the incident. Go back later that day and confront that behavior alone. If the principal blows up again, walk away, record the encounter, and leave a copy in your principal's mailbox. Be as dispassionate and objective as you can. Stick to observable behaviors, add witnesses, if any, and be clinical about your language.

At the very least, confronting and attempting to negotiate behavior modification with a bully allows you to document your attempts to find an in-house solution. Keep complete records of these attempts to use if you bring in your union or federation, go over the principal's head, or file a legal complaint.

Endgame

At some point in your dealings with a bully, you may realize that the two of you alone are not going to settle the issues that stand between you. You still have options that will allow you control the situation and the outcome. Decide beforehand what it will take to settle the conflict. You may want prescribed limits on the principal's behavior toward you while you remain at the school, you may want assurances that the principal's behavior toward other staff and students will be monitored, or you may demand a transfer to a comparable position at another school. At the very least, you will be able to escape the bully's clutches; just don't expect an apology, formal or otherwise.

If you haven't already done so, visit your family physician to ask your doctor to document the impact continuing workplace abuse has had on your health. The more ammunition you have, the better, and a doctor's written opinion carries a lot of weight. Require a witness, preferably a union or federation representative, to be present whenever meeting privately with the principal. Arrange a meeting with your principal, your principal's superior, and your union or federation representative to present your well-documented case and your options for resolution. Be firm in your willingness to file a grievance and to continue the fight on up the ladder of responsibility. Be prepared, as well, for the fact that if you remain in the school, so too will the bullying principal.

Containing a bullying principal is an arduous, complex, and daunting proposition; dislodging one is almost impossible. A bullying school will remain just that until a bullying principal leaves. When a collaborative and equity-minded principal takes over a bullying culture, that principal will require everyone's utmost support and cooperation to subdue the adult bullying elements that remain. And the process could take years. In the meantime, teachers try as best they can to create a safe, positive, and bully-free zone in their own classrooms while they negotiate with those elements still compromising the school's integrity — the colleague on hall duty who ignores the constant student–student bullying, the vice-principal who is reluctant to enforce the anti-bullying rules, the parent swearing with impunity at the school secretary.

The lessons learned from dealing with bullying adults in a school should inform your work to eradicate student bullying. When mature, experienced, confident adults have such a tough time resolving bullying situations, is it any wonder that students struggle with the same problems? While bullying students form the largest tier in a bullying culture, remember that they are the symptom of a bullying culture in schools, and not the root cause.

3

The Bullying School

The bullying dynamic is complex and multidimensional. The search for simple solutions to a complex problem has led to the growth of a number of myths about school bullying.

Teachers, parents, and the public at large are often misled by these myths. Many people both inside and outside the profession, for example, believe that only certain kinds of schools are subject to widespread student–student bullying. They mistakenly assume that bullying plagues only schools in lower socio-economic areas or schools with poor academic records. The research indicates otherwise. Student–student bullying can be a major problem in any school, anywhere. The one factor determining the amount of student–student bullying is the school's culture: the key factor in a school's culture is the degree of commitment among the staff to do something about bullying. Commitment influences behavior. That kind of commitment is dependent on a number of variables, such as

- the attitude of staff members toward student–student bullying
- the number of bullies on staff
- the degree of collaboration among staff members
- the amount of small-group cooperative learning employed throughout the school
- the degree to which staff monitors academic and social progress

> **The one factor determining the amount of student–student bullying is the school's culture: the key factor in a school's culture is the degree of commitment among the staff to do something about bullying.**

The Bullying School Culture

Some principals are reluctant to believe they have a problem in their schools, and actually set up roadblocks to anti-bullying programs. If there is some evidence of student–student bullying, it's excused as to be expected. They allocate few resources or time to the issue and, if there is a policy, they regularly treat student bullies more leniently or in a way different from what the policy dictates.

The Parent as Bully

Boards of education and teachers' unions are raising the alarm about a surprising twist to the issue of bullying — the rise of *parental* bullying in schools. Parents are accosting the school secretary, the principal, and classroom teachers, often in front of children, to vent their rage at what they consider to be unfair marking or discipline. Student–student bullying is a particularly sensitive issue. Parents of both bully and target are often inflamed by, respectively, too harsh or too lenient penalties for bullying.

> **In a nationwide poll of school violence, the Canadian Teachers' Federation discovered that 23% of principals in 2001 had witnessed a parent physically assault or intimidate a teacher.**

The *Toronto Star* reported in a February 2005 article that two Toronto schools had asked parents to shut down Internet chat rooms set up to hold daily teacher-bashing sessions. The same article revealed that Ontario teachers' unions were preparing a survey of public and private schools to determine the extent to which teachers were being bullied and harassed by both students and parents. The National Education Association in the United States estimates that 6250 teachers are physically threatened every day. In a nationwide poll of school violence, the Canadian Teachers' Federation discovered that 23% of principals in 2001 had witnessed a parent physically assault or intimidate a teacher.

Bullying within the System

Highly aggressive individuals — adults or children — who lie, subvert the rules, compete unfairly for personal gain, or abuse the power they hold over others are like wolves in a sheep pen.

While school boards and teachers' unions are quick to point fingers at parents who bully in the schools, they have suspiciously little to say about teachers and administrators who bully. Nevertheless, the word is getting out. According to studies by Dr. Charol Shakeshaft of Hofstra University in Hempstead, New York, a full 15% of all students will be abused by a teacher before they graduate. An international 1995 study examined a large number of seven- and eight-year-olds, and discovered that 15% had witnessed bullying in school by an adult. In a 1993 study, "Hostile Hallways," the authors reported that 18% of the students they surveyed had experienced in-school sexual harassment by a school employee. When Dr. Stuart Twemlow of The Peaceful Schools Project in Houston, Texas, surveyed a large number of teachers, 25% of those teachers admitted to bullying at least a few times and 2% actually admitted to frequent bullying. In several Canadian studies, including one in which school playgrounds were videotaped, teachers on yard duty seemed to be aware of only a small percentage of bullying incidents; in those incidents they did observe, they intervened a little more than 20% of the time. Overall, it seems that teachers intervene in bullying less than 10% of the time.

And what about the behavior of principals, vice-principals, and other administrators? If little data has been gathered about teacher–student bullying behavior, the bullying behavior of administrators remains almost completely obscured. We can, on the other hand, make a few well-educated guesses. A great deal of research has been conducted over the past decade into bullying in the workplace. This focus on adults bullying adults sheds considerable light on what is probably going on in schools.

Researchers Gary and Ruth Namie, for example, have discovered that bullying affects one in six workers in the U.S. and that 81% of bullies are bosses. Apply those numbers to a school or a school district and the implications are disquieting. The research on adult workplace bullying indicates that the bully is usually in a superior position, sometimes a co-worker, and occasionally someone from a lower position. The Namies have set up a bullying hotline for targets of bullying bosses: the two occupations most frequently calling the hotline are nurses and teachers.

If applied to a school, these statistics and concepts suggest that a principal, vice-principal, department head, or someone in a position of responsibility would be most liable to bully others, such as teachers, office personnel, students, or parents. Following this template, teachers might also be targeted by other teachers, occasionally by parents, custodial staff, and even students. Students, of course, are on the bottom rung of the school pecking order and could be targeted by other students, the teacher, the principal or vice-principal, or even the office or custodial staff.

- A principal, vice-principal, or department head would be most likely to bully others, such as teachers, office personnel, students, or parents.
- Teachers might also be targeted by other teachers, occasionally by parents, custodial staff, and even students.
- Students could be targeted by other students, the teacher, the principal or vice-principal, or even the office or custodial staff.

To this point, research into bullying has centred on two distinct environments. Childhood bullying is studied in schools; adult bullying is studied in the workplace. But what if your workplace is the school? Schools bring large numbers of children together each day in one building and place them under the care and control of a designated group of adults. We expect these adults to act responsibly, wisely, fairly, and compassionately. We also expect them at all times to maintain high moral and ethical standards and to model the attitudes and behaviors we expect children to develop. That's a tall order for anyone to fill. The wonder is that so many of our educators serving in schools genuinely possess those values and display those characteristics day after day. The uncomfortable truth is that not all do.

Teachers and students are vulnerable to bullying in schools for similar reasons. We expect a school to be a refuge from the outside world, a place where everyone is kept physically and emotionally safe and secure. Schools are responsible for inculcating the basic values of a society and, in fact, are supposed to mirror in microcosm how these values benefit both the society and the individual. In a school, everyone is expected to tell the truth, to follow the rules, to cooperate with each other for the good of all, and to accede to the decisions of authority figures. Highly aggressive individuals — adults or children — who lie, subvert the rules, compete unfairly for personal gain, or abuse the power they hold over others are like wolves in a sheep pen.

The first step in controlling and treating bullying in a school environment is acknowledging that anyone in the building, especially the adults who are acting as surrogate parents, can bully and be bullied. How effective can any zero-tolerance policy be if students are expected to believe in anti-bullying ideals while witnessing adults around them bullying others and being bullied themselves? Any anti-bullying policy based on the assumption that students will do as teachers say and not as they do will accomplish nothing. How diligent will teachers be in implementing their school's anti-bullying strategies while under the thumb of a bullying principal? How effective can any bullying policy be if it's applied piecemeal, subjectively and inconsistently?

Principals can be bullies; teachers can be bullies; and so can parents. And if adult bullying stains a school, wiping out student bullying is an uphill battle. If a school is developing or has developed a bullying culture, the effects are wide-ranging and invidious. Keep in mind that that the majority of adults in any school are idealistic, hard-working, nurturing professionals who accept their vocation as a calling rather than as a job. A few key individuals, however, wielding and abusing whatever power they possess, can turn a school into a toxic environment.

From the extreme example in the box on the next page, it's clear that a bullying school culture defies easy or simple analysis. It's not simply a matter of a principal bullying a teacher who then bullies students. If the dynamic were as linear as the classic case of a parent slapping a child who then turns to slap the family dog, intervention would be more clear-cut and definitive. In a bullying school, the student who is bullied at home is likely to bully other students at school; that same student might also try to bully the teacher using the reputation of the bullying parent as leverage. A collaborative, fair-minded principal might inadvertently empower a bullying teacher, who might use that leverage to bully other teachers as well as students. Teachers who band together to stand up against a bullying principal might well find themselves undermined by the principal's superior or even by the school community.

Once bullying compromises a school's integrity, students bear the brunt of the failure. Bullying principals, teachers, and students directly inflict needless and inexcusable suffering in targeted students. By themselves, bullying principals can tip a school into a downward spiral by modeling and enabling bullying behavior among staff and students. Bullying principals and teachers target and aggress against selected staff and parents; in the process they undermine, discredit, and disable the staff commitment essential for the success of an anti-bullying program. Left unchecked, bullying parents contribute to the poisoned environment by coercing staff and subverting the orderly functioning of the school.

In a bullying school, morale is eroded, initiative squelched, and risk-taking discouraged. Apprehension seeps into the learning environment. Adults, as well as students, are reluctant to take risks or make mistakes for fear of ridicule or censure. People feel alienated, isolated, and disenfranchised and begin to mistrust their own abilities and competencies. As they fall prey to dependence, ignorance, and uncertainty, their capacity to learn or teach is critically impaired. As the bullying in a school increases, a school's effectiveness wanes.

As the bullying in a school increases, a school's effectiveness wanes.

A Visit to your Worst Nightmare

Imagine that you're filling in for a Grade 5 teacher who may be off for a few weeks. It's your first day on the job. You report to the office.

Welcome to Watchyerstep Public School. I'm Doris, the head secretary. I think you'll like it here; it's a good school. I do like the morning attendance sheets sent down promptly; I'd hate to have to embarrass you on the "on-call." The office photocopier is off-limits to teachers no matter how many others in the school have broken down. We're busy here and we don't have time to wait in line. And don't send kids down to the office and expect us to watch them. We have more than enough to do as it is.

I'd introduce you to the principal but her door is closed this morning. After a while you'll get used to figuring out the best time to talk to her. You'll like her though: she's tough but fair. She's usually pretty busy, so I wouldn't bother her unless it's really important. If it has anything to do with ordering books or supplies, or spending money at all, just give the request to me in writing and I'll see what I can do. You don't want to get on her bad side.

That made you jump, didn't it? You'll get used to it. It's just Dave, the VP. He's in charge of discipline and one of the school bullies was sent in early from the yard for fighting. Dave will rip into him like that for a bit, tear a strip off his back, and the kid will leave bawling his eyes out. Dave has a knack for it. He'll go after the odd teacher now and then, but it's just for their own good. We like to run a tight ship around here. You'll really like him. He has a new joke every day and some of them will make your hair curl. Just don't get caught in the book room with him, if you know what I mean.

That's Sonja, the other Grade 5 teacher. You'll be teaching across the hall from her. She's a terrific teacher. You can go by her classroom any time you like and you won't hear a peep. Her kids do as they're told if they know what's good for them. She'll tell you what texts to use and fill you in on the routines. Follow her lead and you won't have any problems.

Speaking of problems, you have the Robertson boy in your class. He's a bit of a rough-and-tumbler, but it's the other kids who mostly get him into trouble. Some of them egg him on; you know, they just ask for it. Anyway, I'd go easy on him; his mother can get a little out of hand. She went after the teacher you're replacing and the principal in the hall last week, just when the classes were changing. You should have heard the language! She's also not afraid to call the area superintendent over the least little thing. You'll say something to the boy, the boy tells her, she phones the superintendent, the super calls the principal, and the next thing you know you're hauled up on the carpet. It might also be a good idea to check the kind of marks the boy usually gets before you mark any work, if you know what I mean.

Anyway, I'd like to talk to you for a while longer but we're really busy here in the office. But I can tell right off that you're the kind of teacher we need here in Watchyerstep P.S.

School Assessment

The survey at the end of the chapter (pages 70 to 73) affords you the opportunity to take an objective and critical look at your school culture and the state of bullying within that culture.

Every school has shone the spotlight on student–student bullying at some time and in some manner. What usually happens, however, is that the spotlight shifts relatively quickly to a fresh school objective, and staff and students focus their attentions elsewhere. Even if an emphasis on anti-bullying is maintained, it's difficult to create change on a schoolwide basis. Schools rarely manifest a single, homogeneous culture; a typical school will contain two, three, or more cliques comprised of teachers with similar beliefs, attitudes, and methods. The strongest of these cliques usually sets the tone for the school. Their influence is so powerful that, even when teachers are withdrawn from a school for intensive in-servicing in an opposing viewpoint, they will revert to past attitudes once they're re-immersed in the school culture with which they identify.

The survey at the end of this chapter (pages 70 to 73) affords you the opportunity to take an objective and critical look at your school culture and the state of bullying within that culture. It is divided into five sections: your answers will allow you to focus on specific implementation areas and to identify problematic items within each of the areas.

- Section A allows you to determine the general school tone. The items help you assess the manner in which students and adults interact with one another on a daily basis. As you reflect on the items, imagine the impressions a stranger walking around the school would form.
- Section B identifies the nature and extent of your school's formal anti-bullying policy. Some of the items require an action or a planned action in the present term or school year. It's not enough that these steps were taken last year. To be effective, the policy has to be cyclically renewed.
- Section C addresses how effectively the anti-bullying policy is implemented. Although the staff should be in-serviced on student and adult bullying on a yearly basis, schools don't have the luxury of that kind of time. On the other hand, with the natural movement of teachers from school to school and the constant wave of implementation projects within a school, in-servicing needs to be revisited regularly to ensure that the importance of anti-bullying strategy is always front and centre.

- Section D asks you how and how often the state of bullying is evaluated in your school. If schools don't establish a baseline by surveying all affected parties, and compare the progress of anti-bullying measures each year against that baseline, their efforts are bound to fail.
- Section E establishes the extent to which the groups in your school are collaborating with one another. A collaborative culture fosters an open and equitable environment. As they work together as a team, students, parents, and teachers earn each other's trust and respect. In a collaborative environment, bullying of any sort is never tolerated.

Although bullying is artificially separated into sections in the survey, be assured that behavior in one area affects behavior in another. In actual practice, all five areas are intimately interrelated.

As you reflect on the results of the survey, the patterns that emerge are more instructive than the raw scores. If you find that you can agree or strongly agree with most of the items in most of the sections, you can be assured that you're part of an effectively functioning, anti-bullying school. If you disagree or strongly disagree with many of the items in several of the categories, you will conversely understand where your school needs to focus its anti-bullying efforts. Should you find that you disagree or strongly disagree with most of the items in most of the categories, you will clearly understand the magnitude of your school's bullying culture. Depending on your position in the school and the strength of your allies, you will also have a better idea of how successfully you can advocate for change. To better understand that change process, it's essential to look at the school population not as members of groups but as individuals.

The Schoolhouse Biosphere

Bullying in schools can only be understood in the context of a school's unique environment. Except for schools and prisons, our society seldom forcibly confines large numbers of people in a single building for long periods of time. Students have no voice in choosing with whom they go to school, what they do at the school, or who the adults are who have total authority over them. This captive audience is subjected to the bullying that goes on in and around schools with one less option than adults have: they can't just leave.

As you examine each of the elements in the schoolhouse biosphere, you come to realize how bullying can stem from and be compounded by the intrinsic nature of each layer.

On the surface, a school's structure suggests that the adults in charge are well able to carefully supervise and strictly regulate the behavior of the student population. Each teacher is directly responsible for the behavior of a classroom of students, common areas are patrolled on a regular basis, and a principal oversees the functioning of the entire building. As you examine each of the elements in the schoolhouse biosphere, however, you come to realize how bullying can stem from and be compounded by the intrinsic nature of each layer.

Student Diversity

At the core of the educational environment, of course, are the students. From the outside, it appears that students have few opportunities to deviate from the codes of behavior laid out for them or from the adult surveillance that enforces those behaviors. Nothing can be further from the truth. Just as convicts do in prisons, students create a subculture specific to each institution and its population that exists parallel to the official structure. That subculture is built on a foundation of friendship, status, and the values of the in-crowd, and gives rise to a maze of peculiar customs, cliques, codes, and jargon.

Individual students share a range of characteristics that shift and change according to the dictates of the lives they're leading. A one-size-fits-all approach to curriculum or discipline stems from the fantasy that all students are fundamentally alike. They aren't. To grasp what's involved in interpreting, managing, and influencing behavior in a classroom or school, consider this description (from *Response Journals Revisited*) of the daunting complexity of a school's clients.

> Students appear in different sizes and shapes and vary in physical, social, emotional, and intellectual development. They come from diverse socio-economic backgrounds, from many countries and cultures, and operate in English as their first, second, or third language. Some are gregarious; some seldom speak.
>
> Students belong to different sorts of families. Some come from one- and two-parent families; some are in foster homes, some in group homes. Some have a parent or guardian waiting for them when they arrive home from school; some are latch-key kids. Some have strong religious beliefs and some have no religion at all. One in ten is gay, lesbian, or bisexual.
>
> Their intelligences vary. On standardized tests, including intelligence tests, some score very low and some very high, and most are strung out somewhere in-between. Some show immediate aptitude for mathematical concepts; some have difficulty with simple arithmetic. Some have difficulty reading in high school, while some have been reading fluently since before they started Kindergarten.
>
> Their strengths and needs differ. Most are reasonably healthy; some are chronically ill. Some are admired athletes; some are scorned losers. Some are abused at home; some are enriched. Some have special gifts; some have special needs. Some thrive in the school environment; some fail day after day.
>
> Students are nourished and nurtured differently. Most had breakfast this morning; some didn't. Some were hugged before they came to school; some were beaten. They all laugh, at times, and some cry. Some readily share their joy and grief, pleasure and pain, their frivolous enthusiasms, and their terrible secrets; some keep everything locked up inside.
>
> All live intimate, intensely felt lives in which social concerns and pressures are paramount.

Within this incredible diversity lie the seeds of bullying. Some students arrive at school with aggression already programmed as their primary coping mechanism; some learn aggression within the school's cauldron of risk-taking and frustration, success and failure, acceptance and rejection. All students attempt to cope with the physical, social, emotional, and intellectual pressures as best they can. Some become bullies; some are targeted by bullies; and many stand witness to the damage bullies do.

Teacher Diversity

The adults in the school create their own subculture, based on a complicated web of power dynamics and friendship, structured according to a well-defined pecking order, and containing well-insulated cliques. Schools can be viewed as the interdependent interaction of these two subcultures, student and adult, complex in themselves and exponentially complex in their interactions. In order to fully

A one-size-fits-all approach to curriculum or discipline stems from the fantasy that all students are fundamentally alike. They aren't.

apprehend and attend to bullying, you have to understand and appreciate the diversity of the individuals who make up each of these worlds.

Responsibility for confronting, sorting out, and managing the thousands of student interactions each day lies directly with the teachers. Too often we talk about teachers as if they were all clones of an archetype, imbued with the same experiences, values, personalities, skills, and motivations. We talk about teachers implementing a specific curricular initiative, such as an anti-bullying policy, as if they act and react with one mind and one will. The opposite, of course, is true.

Just like students, teachers come in all shapes and sizes, and vary in social, emotional, and intellectual development. They also possess different areas of expertise. Most are expected to teach any and all subjects in the curriculum regardless of their expertise; some are subject-specific specialists. Teachers also vary in teaching experience: some are in their first year of teaching, some are in their last, and the rest are strung in-between. Regardless of teacher training or formal in-servicing, most revert to teaching the way they were taught when they were in school or the way their immediate colleagues taught in their first teaching assignment. Many are content to remain classroom teachers; some are highly ambitious and aspire to leadership positions. Many regard teaching as a calling; some see it as a job.

In spite of vision statements from school boards, curricular guidelines, and directives, teachers have their own ideas about what's supposed to happen in classrooms and how students should behave. In some cases, this insular subjectivity ensures that quality education endures in the face of the latest, politically motivated, "flavor of the month" initiative; in other cases, it undermines and subverts essential change.

Teachers exercise considerable latitude in how they organize and manage their classrooms. Some view themselves as "the sage on the stage," while others are more comfortable as the "guide on the side." Some emphasize cooperation and collaboration among their students; some foster intense competition. Some encourage students to talk to one another as they work; others insist on a quiet classroom at all times. Some constantly yell; others seldom raise their voices. Some use put-downs, sarcasm, threats, and intimidation; most treat students with respect and understanding.

As with people in any occupation, teachers experience different degrees of contentment in their personal lives. They may come to school at peace with themselves and all around them, they may be depressed and despondent, or they may feel frustrated and angry. A few have problems with drugs, alcohol, or anger management. Some have strong religious beliefs and some have no religion at all. One in ten is gay, lesbian, or bisexual.

Teachers disagree about their professional duties and responsibilities. Some feel they teach a subject that students either learn or not; others feel they teach children and that subject matter is secondary. Some feel it's essential to involve themselves in their students' personal lives; others feel that's the parents' responsibility. Some take responsibility only for the students in their classrooms; some assume responsibility for students wherever they meet them. Some challenge racist, sexist, or homophobic language any time they hear it anywhere in the school; others turn a deaf ear even in their own classrooms. Most are usually on time for supervisory duties; some are chronically late.

All teachers live intimate, intensely felt lives in which collegial, interpersonal, or administrative concerns and pressures often add to the concerns and pressures arising from the classroom. Further complicating their responses to the bullying that goes on among their students are the roles they themselves may be assuming

Just like students, teachers come in all shapes and sizes, and vary in social, emotional, and intellectual development. They also possess different areas of expertise.

in their adult relationships within the school under the eye and control of the school leadership. With teachers, some are bullies; some are targets; and many are bystanders as both students and colleagues are bullied.

Principal Diversity

The attitudes, beliefs, personality, leadership style, and motivations of the principal further complicate and affect how students and adults interact within the school environment and how bullying is perceived and managed.

Dominating both student and adult subcultures is the school leadership, under the control and direction of the principal. In the complex worlds of student and teacher, everyone accepts that the boss of the school is the principal. The attitudes, beliefs, personality, leadership style, and motivations of the principal further complicate and affect how students and adults interact within the school environment and how bullying is perceived and managed. Keep in mind that principals are promoted through the ranks; the values, beliefs, behaviors, and personalities they displayed as teachers follow them into their leadership roles. The crucial difference is that they now can indulge their personal quirks and idiosyncrasies without fear of censure. They're now the bosses.

Principals vary in the interpersonal and management skills required of a leader and in their perceptions of the role of principal. While principals have to attend to the dictates of their superiors and the educational goals established through the political process, they possess considerable latitude in how they view their role as principal and how they go about managing their schools. Some principals, for example, see themselves primarily as business managers and pay little attention to what goes on in classrooms; others see themselves as lead teachers, whose primary responsibilities are the delivery of curriculum and the teaching of teachers. Some principals are naturally collaborative and easily delegate authority; others are highly autocratic and micromanage every aspect of the school. Most allocate resources to best serve the needs of their students; some treat school funds as the source of their power, distributing money to best serve their own personal agendas. Some are gifted motivators; some are feared intimidators; most are decent people trying to do an exacting and frustrating job.

Some principals have an open-door policy and are highly visible throughout the school; they share in supervisory duties and extra-curricular activities, and their paperwork often goes home with them at the end of the day. Others sit behind closed doors, enjoying the fruits of their position and making sure their paperwork is finished and their hands empty by the 3:30 bell. Some keep reminding their staffs how busy they are and how difficult their job is; others remember their days in the classroom and constantly strive to ease the burden of their overworked teachers. Some immerse themselves in the lives of their students and staff; others keep everyone at arm's length and look forward to their next promotion.

All power corrupts and absolute power corrupts absolutely. Bullying hinges on a power imbalance. Principals wield the same uncomfortable power over everyone in their schools as teachers wield in their classrooms. In effective schools, principals ignore the lure of power and strive to empower others to keep finding solutions to the thorniest of problems, including bullying. In bullying schools, the principal is often the source of the problem.

The Search for a Cure

When schools implement anti-bullying programs, the programs focus only on student–student bullying. All schools seem to go through a similar process when implementing their anti-bullying programs. First is the fact-finding and educational stage. Staff and students are surveyed to discover the extent of the student–student bullying problem; staff are in-serviced on student bullying behavior in general and on the specific anti-bullying approach about to be introduced. The school then promotes the program. The community is informed through an information meeting and a written notice at the same time the staff takes the content to the students.

Depending on the age of the students and the particular type of anti-bullying program, that content might include a clear articulation of negative behaviors and their consequences; strategies for bullies, such as impulse control, anger management, and developing empathy for others; and adult-led talk-therapy sessions for targets. These approaches are usually preceded by a classroom blitz on bullying in guidance or health classes. Classroom teachers, aided by guidance personnel or social workers, deliver a series of prepackaged anti-bullying lessons designed to outline for all students the dangers of bullying and the prosocial choices that support positive peer interactions. As the program is implemented, teachers increase their vigilance, and cases of student–student bullying are summarily dealt with.

Schools seem to favor one of three types of anti-bullying programs. The most common and least successful approach is a zero-tolerance program that implements an established and escalating series of sanctions or consequences if rules are broken. The consequences range from detentions to suspensions. School boards like this approach for several reasons: it fits the crime-and-punishment pattern with which the community is familiar; it can be written down and implemented in the same way in every school; in cases in which bullying in a school has an extreme or tragic outcome, the school and board can point to a concrete program as a legal defence against negligence.

Another widely used approach revolves around some form of problem solving. The students involved in a bullying episode are led through a process designed to promote understanding and empathy for all concerned. This type of intervention highlights why everyone acted as they did and encourages students to develop prosocial options for future behavior. This approach recognizes the dynamic of bully–target–bystander and attempts to address motivations and behavior in a relatively non-judgmental manner. Putting this theory into practice can be problematic. Developing empathy in bullies, especially when they are older students, is a chancy proposition, and convincing bystanders to intervene is equally perplexing. Since bullying hinges on a power imbalance, putting a target face-to-face with a bully simply reintroduces that power imbalance in a different context. Too often, schools with an existing conflict-resolution program involving peer mediation simply fold bullying situations into the same program. When the conflict involves a power imbalance, peer facilitators lack the insight, experience, and authority to equitably resolve bullying.

The third approach tends to merge the other two approaches, diverting less severe cases into a problem-solving mode and addressing more serious cases with sanctions.

The critical flaw of these types of approach to anti-bullying lies not in the programs themselves, but in the fact that they are grafted onto whatever else is going on in the school. Anti-bullying programs that are implemented from outside the school curriculum are doomed to follow all the other innovations that flare for a moment in a school's consciousness and then die away from lack of attention. Anti-bullying has to grow from the inside out, as part of the foundation on which

Schools seem to favor one of three types of anti-bullying programs:

- **a zero-tolerance program that implements an established and escalating series of sanctions if rules are broken**
- **a problem-solving process designed to promote understanding and empathy**
- **a combination of the above**

The critical flaw of these types of approach lies in the fact that they are grafted onto whatever else is going on in the school.

the curriculum is built. It has to be inherent in the fundamental principles that define all relationships in any school. And it has to apply to students and adults equally.

An Anti-bullying Blueprint

Bullies don't know that they're bullies: they're simply people who are attempting to understand and cope with the world around them as best they can. For any number of reasons, they've misread and misinterpreted the prosocial dynamics of interpersonal behavior. Rationalization and self-justification obscure bullies' self-awareness to the point where they have inordinate difficulty recognizing and acknowledging their bullying behavior. They see punishment as fundamentally unfair and unreasonable: why would someone with power aggress against them just because they aggressed against someone else? Punishment in and of itself simply reinforces their intrinsic belief that power and aggression are the essential and controlling values in a society. Inconsistencies in the school environment merely substantiate this tragic misapprehension.

Student bullies thrive on inconsistency. If they can point to a discrepancy in values from classroom to classroom, from principal to teacher, or from year to year, it fortifies their own sense that values are a relative commodity. Bullies feel that they're doing what everyone else would do if they had the courage, strength, confidence, or intelligence. However, the more that bullies find their own attitudes and actions at odds with those of everyone else around them, the more uncomfortable and insecure they become about their personal convictions. If bullies encounter dissonance wherever they turn in an environment, they are effectively neutralized.

Consistency in education is hard to come by. Schools are buffeted by constant change. Students, parents, staff, and curricular priorities are shifting variables that constantly reformulate and redefine a school's character. If a school community that has worked tirelessly toward creating a bully-free environment suffers an adverse change in school administration and sees key staff members transfer out, it will within a year find itself back at square one, with a vicious bullying problem on its hands. For a school to successfully combat bullying, certain basic values have to be recognized, implemented, and respected by everyone in the building, including administration, teachers, office staff, and visiting parents. That's why all schools need to go through a process of renewed commitment to anti-bullying each and every year.

The foundation of any anti-bullying policy is the belief in cooperation for the good of all, and in respect for self, peers, and students. That same belief lies at the heart of the learning/teaching process. Regardless of grade level, subject area, or course content, learning is maximized if students feel physically and psychologically safe in the environment and valued by their peers and adults. Teachers can effectively understand, direct, cope with, and resolve the physical, emotional, and intellectual needs of thirty or more students only if they themselves feel physically and psychologically safe in the environment and valued by their peers and by the administration. Schools must operate as bully-free zones for students and staff alike. Double standards in that regard will erode the moral center of any school, place students and staff in jeopardy, and cripple the learning/teaching process.

Punishment in and of itself simply reinforces a bully's intrinsic belief that power and aggression are the essential and controlling values in a society.

For a school to successfully combat bullying, certain basic values have to be recognized, implemented, and respected by everyone in the building, including administration, teachers, office staff, and visiting parents.

67

The following questions ask you to reflect on the current state of your school's anti-bullying environment. With the values embedded in these questions firmly in place in your school, any firm commitment to anti-bullying will produce dramatic results. If these values are inconsistently represented in your school, no official anti-bullying policy will succeed for long. If you can't answer in the affirmative to these questions, your school needs a major moral overhaul.

- *Does your school staff insist on an environment completely free of sexist, racial, cultural, ability-related, and homophobic stereotyping?*

The gym teacher who tells a student he's "playing like a little girl," the yard duty teacher who turns a deaf ear as students call each other "faggot," and the principal who insists that bullying just isn't a problem in a higher socio-economic setting are all aiding and abetting bullying. The only way to maintain a school culture resistant to bullying is to insist on equity for everyone. In this environment, all adults are keenly aware that they serve as models for their students, displaying, for example, a genuine courtesy toward others and a respect for individual differences.

Double standards are insidious and corrosive. All adults should interact with each other and with students in a fair, respectful, and equitable manner. Teachers who berate and humiliate students shouldn't be surprised when some students follow their lead and berate and humiliate other students. Administrators model the behavior they expect from their teachers, and teachers model the behavior they expect from students — even when students aren't present. Private spaces don't exist in a school. The principal or teacher telling sexist or homophobic jokes in the office or lunchroom is undermining a school's consensus on equity, breaching school and board policy, and poisoning the environment. Bigotry and bullying go hand in hand.

- *Do all teachers display a respectful attitude toward all students and a genuine regard for their learning?*

All students have the right to be respected and to learn: the two are intertwined. The most important variable in the learning process is an individual's sense of self-worth. Learning requires risk-taking; risk-taking requires a healthy sense of self-worth. Bullying not only destroys the self-esteem of targets but also casts a cloud of uncertainty and insecurity over the entire learning environment. The needs of learners clash directly with the tyrannical personality of the bully. What people say and how they say it, what they do, even the way they look or dress can attract a bully's attention and turn someone into a target. The damage that student bullies do to the learning environment is significant; the damage that adult bullies do is catastrophic.

Regardless of disability, gender, sexual orientation, race, ethnocultural origin, faith, or socio-economic status, all students must be empowered to learn through positive reinforcement, the understanding and acceptance of individual differences, and the encouragement of trial and error. Mistakes especially must be welcomed and affirmed as an authentic component of the learning process. Remarks like "That was a stupid question" or "You're just being lazy" are rooted in ignorance, perpetuated by abuse of power, and antithetical to the learning process. Some students turn to bullying when their frustrations with learning erode their self-esteem. When all student learning is valued and facilitated, those frustrations are diverted before they build.

- *Do all teachers in the school use cooperative learning strategies?*

What does a learning/teaching strategy have to do with bullying? Frustration with learning, poor self-esteem, and inadequate social skills all often contribute to student–student bullying behaviors. In small-group discussions, students interact with and learn from one another. Cooperative learning strategies, which stress peer collaboration, have been shown to contribute to higher academic achievement, to increase self-esteem, to improve social skills, and to facilitate language development. They can be used effectively with all age groups and in any subject area. As well as contributing to a wide range of intellectual goals, these small-group instructional techniques involve process skills that help teachers counter bias, discrimination, and bigotry of all kinds.

Students who are constantly reacting to decisions others make for them have difficulty accepting responsibility for what goes on in the classroom and school environments. When students have opportunities to collaboratively make decisions and solve problems related to the classroom learning experience, they are more apt to accept responsibility for the social interactions swirling around them. When learning becomes a group problem-solving process, solving racist behavior or homophobic harassment, for example, naturally becomes everyone's responsibility.

- *Are teachers meaningfully involved in the decision-making and problem-solving processes on a schoolwide basis?*

Anti-bullying policies can be imposed from outside the school or created on the inside. Mandated policies, official directives, and perfunctory in-servicing will only turn anti-bullying into another stalled curricular initiative. A commitment to anti-bullying emerges and endures when teachers are convinced that they have a stake in how a school operates. Ownership for an anti-bullying policy begins to take hold when teachers believe that what happens in other classrooms, in the hallways, in the lunchroom, and especially in the main office is everybody's business. Rubberstamping the decisions and decrees of an autocratic, authoritarian principal leads to apathy and neglect.

Principals can empower a staff by employing cooperative learning strategies themselves. Establishing timetable, budget, curricular, or health and safety priorities, or developing and implementing behavior codes or disciplinary policies, for example, require the consensus that derives from a collaborative process. In the course of employing cooperative learning strategies with staff to solve real problems, school leaders also value, demonstrate, and encourage the use of these methods throughout the school.

An anti-bullying program can't stop at the schoolhouse door.

Influencing the variables of interpersonal dynamics within a school can have a dramatic impact on a school's bullying culture. But schools are often limited by factors outside their control. School boards, for example, create policies, establish priorities, and make decisions that determine how and to what extent schools are able to change student and adult bullying behaviors. In addition, students go home each day to families, lives, and influences far beyond the reach of schools. They may leave an anti-bullying culture in school and be instantly engulfed in conflicting values coming at them from all sides. An anti-bullying program can't stop at the schoolhouse door. The crucial battle against bullying begins where the values of the school and the outside world meet and sometimes collide.

Bullying and My School:
School Assessment and Reflection Tool

In this reflection survey, please indicate the extent to which you agree or disagree that each statement correctly describes the dominant behavior in your school.

1 = strongly disagree   2 = disagree   3 = agree   4 = strongly agree

A. Determining the school tone

- Staff displays a respectful attitude toward all students.

    1   2   3   4

- Students display a respectful attitude toward all adults.

    1   2   3   4

- Students display a respectful attitude toward one another.

    1   2   3   4

- Administrators seldom display bullying behavior.

    1   2   3   4

- Teachers seldom display bullying behavior.

    1   2   3   4

- Support staff (secretaries, custodians, etc.) seldom display bullying behavior.

    1   2   3   4

- Parents/guardians seldom display bullying behavior when in the school or on school grounds.

    1   2   3   4

- Visiting board personnel (superintendents, trustees, consultants, etc.) seldom display bullying behavior.

    1   2   3   4

- Students seldom display bullying behavior.

    1   2   3   4

B. Identifying school anti-bullying policies

- The school has a written policy regarding bullying.

    1   2   3   4

- A copy of the school's anti-bullying policy has been sent home this year to parents/guardians.

    1   2   3   4

- A parent/guardian information night regarding the school's anti-bullying policy has been held this school year.

    1   2   3   4

- A student assembly regarding the school's anti-bullying policy has been held this school year.

    1   2   3   4

- Teachers have been directed to review the school's anti-bullying policy with their students this term.

    1   2   3   4

- The school's anti-bullying policy clearly states specific sanctions and the specific behaviors that trigger these sanctions.

    1   2   3   4

- The school's anti-bullying approach contains options for some form of anger management, impulse control, and the development of empathy in bullies.

    1   2   3   4

- The school's anti-bullying approach includes some form of adult-led talk-therapy support for targets.

    1   2   3   4

- The school has a written code of behavior regarding electronic communications (computers, text messaging, cell phones) that includes dealing with forms of electronic bullying.

    1   2   3   4

- The written code of behavior regarding electronic bullying has been sent home this year to parents/guardians.

    1   2   3   4

- Students understand the seriousness of electronic bullying.

    1   2   3   4

C. Implementing the anti-bullying policies

- A staff meeting has been held this year to discuss bullying and anti-bullying measures.

    1   2   3   4

- Teaching staff have been in-serviced within the past two years on the nature of student bullying and what to do about it.

    1   2   3   4

- Teaching staff have been in-serviced within the past two years on the nature of adult bullying and what to do about it.

    1   2   3   4

- Administrators agree with all aspects of the anti-bullying policy.

    1   2   3   4

- Administration consistently imposes sanctions for bullying whenever they are warranted.

    1   2   3   4

- Administration correctly uses intervention strategies instead of, or as well as, sanctions when warranted.

    1   2   3   4

- Teachers agree with all aspects of the anti-bullying policy.

    1   2   3   4

- Bullying behavior among students is never tolerated in the classrooms.

    1   2   3   4

- Bullying behavior by and among adults is never tolerated by administration.

    1   2   3   4

- Teachers are on time for their supervisory duties.

    1   2   3   4

- Teachers accept responsibility for supervising all students anywhere in the building or on school grounds.

    1   2   3   4

- Bullying behavior among students is never tolerated anywhere in the building or on school grounds.

    1   2   3   4

- Staff and administration strictly enforce the code of behavior regarding electronic bullying.

    1   2   3   4

D. Evaluating the state of bullying in the school

- The teaching staff was surveyed at some time this year to ascertain the extent and nature of bullying in the school.

    1   2   3   4

- The non-teaching staff was surveyed at some time this year to ascertain the extent and nature of bullying in the school.

    1   2   3   4

- The students were surveyed at some time this year to ascertain the extent and nature of bullying in the school.

    1   2   3   4

- The parents/guardians were surveyed at some time this year to ascertain the extent and nature of bullying in the school.

    1   2   3   4

- The school has some mechanism for determining each year the success of anti-bullying measures.

    1   2   3   4

- A safe, orderly, and equitable environment is maintained throughout the school.

    1   2   3   4

E. Identifying the degree of collaboration within the school

- Administration uses cooperative learning strategies with teachers.

    1   2   3   4

- Teachers use cooperative learning strategies with students.

    1   2   3   4

- Administration and staff work together as a mutually supportive team.

    1   2   3   4

- Teachers have meaningful input into setting the agenda for staff meetings.

    1   2   3   4

- Teachers have meaningful input into budget, timetable, and curricular priorities.

    1   2   3   4

4

The Bullying Society

Bullying is a repeated act against an individual or a series of individuals who fear the bully's power. An imbalance of power exists.

Like it or not, we live in a conflict-filled, competitive world. Superpowers routinely impose their will on second- or third-world countries that are economically, politically, or militarily vulnerable. Multinational corporations with value systems based on corporate profits often clash with national imperatives. Religions vie for moral preeminence, with extreme elements resorting to violence and terror. Business, politics, sports, and the arts are riddled with the language of "winners" and "losers."

Everything and everyone is rated and listed: the stock market keeps track of the daily competition in the business world; elections are no-holds-barred dogfights in which one party is declared victorious and the others defeated; drug testing programs can't keep pace with athletes eager to inject their bodies with whatever chemical it takes to stay on top; newspapers print top-ten lists of the latest entertainments based on how much money they've raked in. We want to know who's hot and who's not: who's richest, sexiest, smartest, most attractive, most popular, best dressed, and most likely to succeed. And a multimillionaire gains notoriety for a short time on television by belligerently yelling at a subordinate, "You're fired!"

Is it any wonder that students are confused about how they should act? Their sports heroes routinely indulge in "trash talking," intimidation, lying, cheating, and even physical violence. Every professional hockey team carries enforcers, low-skill players whose value to the team lies in their ability to physically fight and intimidate the opposition; in professional football, controlled violence fuels every play, and defensive specialists are constantly on a search-and-destroy mission; and soccer matches are routinely disrupted, not by violence on the field but by the violent behavior of goons in the stands. Urban music and music videos are frequently racist, sexist, homophobic, and rooted in the violent values of gang mentality. Those same values are mirrored in the video games students play, the Internet chat rooms and web sites they visit, and the movies they watch. Meanwhile, their own lives are subsumed by the virtual reality of advertising and the siren call of airbrushed images, designer drugs, and fifteen minutes of fame.

People with power don't seem to be bound by the same prosocial rules as everyone else: rudeness, fits of temper, self-centeredness, social excesses, and aggression are routinely practised by the powerful and excused by everyone else.

In Japan, conformity is so valued by society that friends, teachers, and peers band together to bully anyone who stands out or refuses to conform. In 1995, an estimated 60,000 Japanese students were being bullied in this manner, and 30% of truants understandably skipped school to avoid the bullying. In North America, students see the power of physical attractiveness, celebrity, wealth, political influence, physical prowess, privileged occupations, and the majority culture, and they see the licence that power buys. People with power don't seem to be bound by the same prosocial rules as everyone else: rudeness, fits of temper, self-centeredness, social excesses, and aggression are routinely practised by the powerful and excused by everyone else.

Schools sincerely trying to deal with school bullying first have to acknowledge that classrooms don't operate under bell jars and that schools aren't hermetically sealed. What's happening elsewhere in the school influences an individual teacher's anti-bullying efforts: what's happening outside the school influences a school's anti-bullying program. And the area outside the school that most profoundly affects students' behavior is the home.

Outreach into Families

What's happening elsewhere in the school influences an individual teacher's anti-bullying efforts: what's happening outside the school influences a school's anti-bullying program. And the area outside the school that most profoundly affects students' behavior is the home.

Families have several essential roles to play in a whole-school anti-bullying program. Whether or not they have the opportunity to engage in those roles depends on a school's attitude toward collaborating with the home. Teachers and principals admire the notion of creating partnerships with parents and guardians, but they have difficulty turning that belief into practice. Given the constant criticism of education, teachers and principals are frequently torn between avoiding the public's cynical view of education and cultivating the open, trusting dialogue that will allow the school and home to work together to better the lives of students. Although educators believe in collaborative, inclusive school cultures, they too often slip into a beleaguered, fortress mentality.

Research has uncovered that families are pivotal both in the development of aggression in children and in the resolution process for both bully and target. Some children begin their schooling already possessing a bullying mentality. Aggression in the home, a reliance on corporal punishment, a primarily punitive approach to child-rearing, or an inconsistent parenting style, in which expectations are set but seldom followed up on, can all contribute to aggressive, bullying behavior in children. There's some research that suggests that if watching television is substituted for children's interactions with parents, it results in students who are more likely to bully at school. Watching television per se doesn't contribute to these children's behavior, but being removed from their parents' attention does. Positive family interactions and emotional support reduce the risk of anti-social behavior.

Schools can take steps to promote a collaborative, inclusive, anti-bullying environment.

1. **Inform the community**
2. **Consult the community**
3. **Enlist the community**

The bully's parents are also central to the resolution process after a bullying episode. For a bully's behavior to change, the parents must be aware of and understand the significance of their child's actions. They have to willingly become proactive in the resolution process and to genuinely convince their child that no one in their family can involve themselves in certain kinds of behavior. If their parenting style is contributing to the behavior, it has to change. More than that, parents need to demonstrate that they intend to support and protect the target from any future aggression from their own children.

For any anti-bullying program to be effective, parents clearly can't be left on the outside looking in. They have to be fully informed, consulted often, and recognized as equal partners in the anti-bullying process. For their part, schools can take steps to promote a collaborative, inclusive, and anti-bullying environment in the following ways.

1. Inform the Community

Parents need information on the behaviors that constitute student–student bullying, the home factors that contribute to bullying, the warning signs that will help them detect both bully and target, and the actions they can take to stop bullying. Items in the school newsletter are not enough. Schools need to organize informational meetings at school both during the day and in the evening, to provide parents with details about the school's anti-bullying policy and to introduce school and community resource personnel who will support the school's initiatives and assist parents. The resources could include

- police liaison officers
- experts in anti-bullying strategies
- board equity officers
- social service representatives
- children's aid workers
- psychologists
- youth workers
- translators and community liaison personnel

Principals could also include an information item about student–student bullying in the school newsletter each time it comes out, such as brief items about current research or new books to help keep parents up-to-date. If the school serves a diverse community, principals should ensure that the newsletter is translated into all pertinent languages.

2. Consult the Community

Schools should solicit the community's observations, advice, and questions about bullying each year. At the same time the student bullying survey (pages 33 to 37) is completed, schools could send a comparable questionnaire home for parents. The questionnaire items would remind parents of the behaviors that constitute bullying and reinforce the importance of anti-bullying in the school.

Parents can contribute a unique perspective on what they notice around the school and what they hear from their children to fill the gaps in how the school staff is evaluating the situation. Their questions will also indicate the kind of information the school still needs to disseminate. During informal conversations with parent visitors to the school and regular parent council meetings, principals can stay abreast of the community's perception of bullying in the school and the effectiveness of the school's anti-bullying initiatives.

3. Enlist the Community

Partnerships with the community are forged little by little and over time. When parents are welcomed into the school on a daily basis and their participation is valued, collaboration on anti-bullying becomes a natural extension of that partnership. Community members have valuable expertise that can be used throughout the curriculum. Parents are eager to volunteer, not only for fundraising or helping in the library but also in the classrooms. The more parents engage in the school in meaningful activities, the more the division between home and school is blurred.

By the same token, teachers need to reach out to parents for information and advice whenever they're concerned or confused about a student's behavior. Parents feel part of a team effort when they're consulted for their opinions instead of merely being informed when something goes wrong or during report-card periods. Working together, parents and teachers can nip many bullying behaviors in the bud and save children from personal harm. In order to effectively collaborate, however, home and school need to operate on the same set of guiding principles.

Challenging School Leadership

Effective implementation of an anti-bullying policy can happen only in a collaborative culture.

Boards of education and their designated school managers, the principals, share the responsibility for ensuring that their schools are bully-free. Their task begins, not ends, with the creation of an anti-bullying policy. Once that policy is formulated, they need to ensure effective implementation by taking up the following challenges:

- The boards must comprehensively train their principals in detecting the signs of student and adult bullying, understanding the different types of bullying situations, and fulfilling their duties and responsibilities when dealing with these behaviors.
- Principals must pass on this information to their staffs during in-service sessions, and post this information in the office and staff lunchrooms and work areas. As well, principals need to convince staff that preventing student and adult bullying of all kinds is a top and continuing priority in their schools.
- The principal and staff must articulate and come to consensus on an anti-bullying policy for all people in the school, students and adults alike. This policy should specifically mention sexual harassment and homophobic behavior. The policy should be conveyed to parents in the school newsletter, parent council meetings, and special "meet the teacher" evenings. The policy would cover all adult visitors to the school, including board supervisors, trustees, and parents.
- All adults within the building should have full information on Employee Assistance Programs, including services provided and the security of confidential measures.
- Principals should ensure that board and school anti-bullying policies are addressed regularly in staff meetings. Staff should be given frequent opportunities to articulate problems and concerns. At least twice a year, students, staff, and parents should complete anonymous surveys so that principals can gauge the state of bullying in the school and the effectiveness of anti-bullying measures.
- Principals must promote honest, frank, and unrestricted communication between themselves and all members of staff. If a principal is too busy to talk with staff and listen to their concerns on a daily basis, people will feel neglected, rejected, and unwilling to team with the principal to challenge hostile and aggressive behaviors throughout the school.
- Principals must be seen to care about all members of their staffs as individuals. If principals are caring, nurturing, and supportive, members of staff are more likely to exhibit those qualities with others. Within a caring environment, principals and teachers do not bully anyone.

Boards and their principals must be sincerely committed to building partnerships. Everybody admires the idea of students, principals and teachers, parents and guardians working together in schools in inclusive partnerships. Antibullying programs can be effectively implemented only in such a collaborative culture.

But building inclusive partnerships isn't easy. Parents and the public at large are wary of the public school system. Some recoil from their own memories of their own school years; some are swayed by the recurrent waves of political teacher-bashing; some parents with children in special need are frustrated by the dichotomy between the accessibility of classroom teachers and the almost impenetrable layers of school bureaucracy that guard a system's resources. Standardized test scores, the rating of schools, salary negotiations and work stoppages, and constant curricular reviews are other issues that create tension between schools and their clients. Mistrust, suspicion, and defensiveness fuel the public's jaundiced view of teachers and the teachers' equally jaundiced view of the public.

The final challenge for a school is breaking down those barriers and forging a genuine partnership with parents and the larger community. The talent, commitment, and enthusiasm parents possess can energize a school. As gatekeepers, principals should be welcoming parents into their schools in every conceivable capacity, from volunteering in classrooms and libraries, to fundraising, to providing expertise for specialized programming. With students, teachers, and parents working collaboratively under one roof in an atmosphere of trust and respect, bullies have no context for their self-centered attitudes and no arena for antisocial behavior.

Commitment, like change, develops in a school over time through a recurrent process of shared reflection. The more principals isolate themselves in their offices and teachers in their classrooms, the more resistant to collaboration they become. But a consensus to stop bullying emerges only through a review of established fundamental values, a renewed commitment to the essential partnership of all stakeholders, and an objective and critical look at the state of your own school's bullying culture.

Bullying and Equity

Bullies justify their behavior in one way or another; that's not surprising. From an early age, children are taught about right and wrong and the concept of fairness. They're given broad basic principles that form the foundation of their value systems, such as "honesty is good" and "all people deserve respect." But our children are always learning from us, even when we don't know we're teaching. They start to figure out that everyone lies and that some kinds of lies are considered worse than others; then the basic principle becomes "honesty is the best policy unless you have a really good reason to lie." That's not how they're taught, of course, but that's the kind of sophisticated distinction many children develop.

Another tenet of society that takes a beating is the concept that all people are deserving of respect, and all people are created equal. One of the first qualifications children learn from the world of professional sports is that all people are deserving of respect except for the people against whom you're competing. They learn to "diss" the opponent as a matter of course. As we begin to pit one student's achievements and abilities against another's — in sports, school, or the arts — the line between competitiveness and aggressiveness becomes similarly blurred.

78

Competitive individuals strive to prove themselves superior to others while respecting the goals and rights of others: aggressive individuals strive to prove themselves superior to others by subjugating them through an unfair or irrational use of power. That's a sophisticated distinction that many adults, let alone young people, have a hard time making

Children become critically confused, however, when they start to qualify the principle that all people are created equal by adding that some people are more equal than others. Therein lies the justification for many bullies to aggress against others. When the concept of universality is broken, exclusion becomes arbitrary. Once children start to believe that all people are created equal except for people of a certain skin color, or a particular religion, or possessing a physical or mental disability, then Pandora's Box is broken wide open. The concept of exclusion is sanctioned.

Researchers have discovered, for instance, that many bullies are also homophobic. Considering the general level of homophobia in North American society, that fact may not be unexpected. But bullies take homophobia one step further. They use homophobic slurs to justify their exclusion of or aggression against anyone they decide to bully, regardless of sexual orientation. Once they label someone, their actions, or their possessions as "gay," they have automatically disempowered and excluded that individual. Once tarnished with a homophobic brush, targets find allies hard to find.

School Boards and Equity

Schools are responsible for inculcating in students the basic values of the society. Those values permeate a school's learning materials, pedagogical practices, assessment instruments, and interactions among all students and adults. A school demonstrates to students in microcosm how and on what basis a society operates and the factors that cause inequity in a society.

Curriculum is commonly defined as everything that happens in a school. That definition needs to be expanded. Since a board's hiring and promotion practices directly affect what happens in a school, they too are essential ingredients in curriculum. For a school to effectively counteract bullying, everything that happens in that school and everyone in that school has to enforce and be protected by a full and functional equity policy.

The claim is often made that schools aren't to blame for the ills of society, nor are they responsible for curing them. The generation attending those schools, however, are the hope for the future; if schools don't adequately prepare students for the task of building a better society, then schools are indeed culpable on both counts. Since bullying is so deeply rooted in discrimination and bigotry, boards of education should be in the vanguard of the struggle for equity. That generally hasn't been the case. Boards of education usually operate with either an incomplete equity policy or a full equity policy they choose to ignore.

To be fair, boards of education don't start out to create a limited or watered down equity policy. In a multicultural society, for instance, discrimination or exclusion on the basis of race, color, culture, ethnicity, or religion is intolerable. These rights are automatically assumed. The rights of the disabled are another matter, not because boards believe in discriminating against them, but because, if boards of education mention disabilities in their official equity policy, they become liable if they don't provide access to their aging buildings and provide the auxiliary services required for the education or employment of the disabled in

For a school to effectively counteract bullying, everything that happens in that school and everyone in that school has to enforce and be protected by a full and functional equity policy.

those buildings. Cash-strapped boards just don't believe they can afford equity for the disabled.

Socio-economic bias creates another problem. One of the peculiarities of standardized tests, for example, is that many of them are skewed in favor of students from middle- and higher-income families. Regardless of the reasons behind this socio-economic advantage, boards see no alternative to the deeply entrenched notion of standardized tests and would prefer not to place an accountability system based on standardized tests under too much scrutiny. If the link between learning in school and nutrition is recognized, for instance, boards would also have to fund school-based breakfast and lunch programs for students from poorer backgrounds.

Other equity issues bring their own peculiar problems. For some conservative boards, gender equity is equated too closely with feminism, and equity of class sounds too much like communism, to generate the backing needed to fit into an equity policy. As far as discrimination on the basis of sexual orientation is concerned, few boards want to touch this "hot potato." By doing so, they would be required to admit and address the widespread homophobia in their schools, at the risk of offending a number of vocal and powerful special interest groups.

A century ago, school boards didn't have to concern themselves with equity in education: they lived in different times and served a different kind of society. The challenge for school boards in the 21st century is twofold. First, they must create official equity policies that ensure that their schools are completely free of sexist, racial, ethnocultural, ability-related, socio-economic, and homophobic stereotyping and biases. But a policy merely gives someone the right to sue and provides a board a legal defence should it be sued.

The second part of the equity challenge is for boards to disseminate and publicize the policy among all members of a school's student body, staff, parents, and community, and to proactively implement such a policy in all schools and for all students and adults under their authority. A fully implemented equity policy provides schools with the prescription they require to adequately deal with the bullying plague. Once the malady is removed from the environment, the disease in individuals becomes easier to cure.

School Boards in Denial

In *The Bully At Work*, the authors establish a measure of the culture of any organization when they declare that good employers purge bullies, and bad ones promote them. School boards do promote bullies. They also protect them. As with promotion in any organization, large or small, who you know can make all the difference. In small boards, favoritism and cronyism handicap the promotion process: adult bullies flourish. In large school boards, sudden expansion in the board interferes with an effective promotional process. When large numbers of principals are needed, aspiring vice-principals who would ordinarily never find themselves on a short list are unexpectedly promoted and tossed into the breach. The larger the school board, as well, the longer the lines of communication, the more distant and impersonal the management style, and the more easily candidates are able to disguise their aggressive tendencies and personality flaws: bullies still flourish, especially if they've chosen the right mentors.

Like all public institutions, school boards have a vested interest in minimizing their problems. The public demands that their tax dollars are spent efficiently and effectively. If a school board began firing principals on a regular basis, they would not only be admitting that their promotion process was critically flawed, but they would also have a more difficult time persuading teachers to leave the safety of tenure for private contracts as principals.

More importantly, given the fact that schools assume responsibility for children's physical and emotional well-being in the absence of their parents and guardians, school boards are reluctant to dig too deeply into their school cultures. If they investigate and discover a problem, the public will begin to question why the system is hiring and promoting bullies. To maintain the public's trust, administrators feel justified in denial. They may have a minor problem with bullying teachers, they'll admit, but certainly never a systemic problem involving principals and their superiors.

Teachers' unions would like to bring the problem of bullying principals into the open for the sake of their members, but are willing to trade off that probe if the issue of bullying teachers is put on the back burner. To do otherwise would be to invite disabling scrutiny of the system, to undermine the credibility and authority of teachers and principals, and to incite chaos in the classroom. Once both boards and unions admit to a bullying problem, they would have to do something about it. Since the more you investigate, the more you find, the byword becomes "don't ask, don't tell."

School Boards: Bullying and Bullied

If the officials of a school board repeatedly rely on an imbalance of power to further their own interests at the expense of their clients' needs, that's bullying. When their clients' interests and their own vested interests diverge, school boards are as prone to bullying as any individual; only the methods differ.

Since bullying is rooted in an imbalance of power, institutions like school boards hold the potential for bullying. The phrase "You can't fight city hall," expresses the sense of impotence individuals feel when they attempt to engage a powerful, implacable, maze-like bureaucracy. Theoretically, school boards serve and are answerable to their clients — students and their parents and guardians. In the course of operating an educational bureaucracy, however, individuals are prone to substitute the goals and needs of the organization for the goals and needs of their clients. Preventing adverse publicity, for example, can take precedence over finding solutions for dangerous asbestos insulation hidden in school walls. If the officials of a school board repeatedly rely on an imbalance of power to further their own interests at the expense of their clients' needs, that's bullying. When their clients' interests and their own vested interests diverge, school boards are as prone to bullying as any individual; only the methods differ.

Since knowledge is power, school boards are instinctively secretive. Politicians had to pass laws, for instance, forcing school boards to publicly share the results of standardized testing. But school boards hoard a host of other secrets, from the number and nature of health hazards in their crumbling schools to the number of grievances filed against their principals. Individual parents with concerns — children with peanut allergies, the aberrations and history of a particular teacher, the number of uncompleted referrals for psychological testing in a board — are forced to engage the board in ignorance.

Once they enter the belly of the beast with a legitimate complaint, parents encounter the labyrinthine machinations of a well-established bureaucracy. They fill out form after form, find themselves shunted from department to department, become entangled in meeting after meeting, resign themselves to constantly expanding deadlines, and endure patronizing, well-oiled excuses. In the process, their concerns and complaints are constantly questioned, downplayed, and dismissed. Time, of course, is an institution's ally. The longer parents spend beating their heads against the institution's walls, the more inclined they are to throw up their hands in frustration and give up. Passive resistance on an institutional scale is an effective management technique.

When problems like student–student bullying in schools garner too much attention and become too large to ignore, ineffective but low-cost solutions, such as zero-tolerance policies, are thrown at the problem and rubberstamped to deflect criticism and lawsuits. Accountability with these programs is minimal. Instead of pre- and post-implementation surveys to measure the success of the initiative, anecdotal evidence from a smattering of principals is used to justify ignoring the ineffectual results.

Policies that would actually make a difference, on the other hand, often never see the light of day. Comprehensive equity policies, for example, can be stalled indefinitely in "public consultations" until the clamor for action dies down or backroom committees render them irrelevant. If a comprehensive policy somehow gets by the school board and is eventually approved, it still has to be implemented. If board officials decide it is too costly, too complicated, or too inconvenient to implement, they surreptitiously send it out to languish and collect dust on principals' bookshelves. When concerned parents or teachers demand equity, the policy is dusted off and waved in their faces. Problem solved.

Keep in mind that parents aren't used to being ignored by the educational system. A fair number of them have found success by bullying their children's teachers and principals. Some parents realize early in their children's school careers that teachers and principals are no different from any other employees: they don't like anyone going over their heads to hassle their bosses. If enough complaints are lodged, bosses start to wonder if there's a fire under all that smoke. Parents also feel entitled to proactively criticize all aspects of a school for three main reasons: they went to school themselves, so they know all about what's right and wrong in education; they pay the teachers' salaries; and, most importantly, they believe that what happens in school directly affects their children's futures.

With that kind of power and motivation behind them, some parents consciously attempt to intimidate anyone and everyone in a school who crosses them. They make constant, harassing phone calls, send abusive notes, demand weekly in-person consultations at unreasonable times, expect daily progress reports, and order a full and immediate accounting, including successful post-test remediation, if their child receives an unsatisfactory mark. They question the teacher's and principal's motives, methods, and values, and blame the school for the child's failure to achieve or behave. They go over the teacher's head to the principal at the slightest provocation, and think nothing of phoning the area's school superintendent to lodge complaints about the teacher and the principal. These bullies are psychologically and sometimes physically intimidating, often loud, offensive, and profane, and completely unpredictable. Too often, their tactics are successful.

This kind of parent may make everyone's lives in a particular school miserable, but any one parent will meet his or her match when attempting to intimidate the officials at the board offices. They simply don't have the clout to disturb a board's monolithic self-interest. Parents who band together, on the other hand, do. If a school seems indifferent to their individual voices, parents in a community sometimes group together to ensure that the school attends to their issues. When their concerns are addressed and taken seriously, these groups are usually agreeable to working together with the school to find equitable solutions.

Groups of parents may legitimately organize to petition for improved services from a school board, addressing such issues as increasing money for textbooks, expanding programs for special-education students, or adding teacher-librarians to the system. Groups that amass power to force practices onto school boards that deny people their basic human rights are another matter. The tactic crosses the line into bullying when special interest groups band together to conduct well-orchestrated media and political campaigns to force school boards to repudiate standard equity policies and practices or to restrict a contemporary syllabus. These groups often conduct religious, racist, or homophobic vendettas to excise curriculum, ban books, or fire or transfer teachers without just cause. When a school board with a siege mentality finds citizen groups working outside the organization's established procedures and publicly storming the barricades, it becomes vulnerable. When groups demand a public accounting, are resistant to bluff, intimidation, or coercion, and are willing to stay the course no matter how long the process takes, school boards need all the friends they can get.

In the case of anti-bullying programs, school boards need to take effective action before the crisis blows up in their faces. They can start by empowering their clients and enlisting their support by dropping the cloak of secrecy and opening up their schools to scrutiny. If they can blanket their schools every year with standardized tests in language and mathematics, for example, they can certainly survey students, parents and guardians, teachers and principals to determine precisely who is bullying whom, how, and how often. With this systemwide report card in hand, they can determine the present state of student and adult bullying, establish goals for anti-bullying programs, and create action plans to achieve those goals. By repeating their surveys at regular intervals, they can evaluate the effectiveness of their anti-bullying efforts and adjust their approach accordingly. This kind of diagnosis, gap analysis, implementation, evaluation, and revision is nothing new. But the success of the approach hinges on first accumulating objective data about all the modes of bullying in schools, no matter how damning that data might be. If school boards truly want to enlist everyone's help in the struggle to eliminate bullying from schools, they have to be willing to engage in objective self-evaluation. The difference between making enemies or creating allies is often the difference between a locked or an open door.

School Boards and Leadership

Teachers already complain about not having enough time to cover the curriculum they have. Add the pressures of standardized testing, gathering marks for report cards, and myriad administrative, supervisory, and extra-curricular demands to the daily grind of preparing and presenting lessons, and they're already running as fast as they can to keep from falling behind. Is anyone really surprised when teachers do the bare minimum as far as classroom anti-bullying teaching is concerned, or turn a blind eye to student–student bullying episodes because they just don't have the time to deal with them?

Parents, teachers, principals, and school boards all agree that anti-bullying programs are essential in order to bring a halt to student–student bullying in schools. An agreement in principle isn't the problem; putting that agreement into practice is. If school boards truly want to make significant inroads into the problem of student–student bullying, they have to find ways to enable their teachers to

If school boards truly want to enlist everyone's help in the struggle to eliminate bullying from schools, they have to be willing to engage in objective self-evaluation.

School boards have to find ways to enable teachers to follow through on their commitment to an anti-bullying program:

- Increasing support personnel and material
- Supporting special programs
- Restructuring curriculum
- Providing leadership

follow through on that commitment. The practical assistance can take many forms.

• *Increasing support personnel and material*

Through cutbacks to education, many schools have lost or reduced to part-time their school nurses, guidance counselors, youth workers, and vice-principals; board psychologists and psychometricians work on a quota system and make learning disabilities a priority; subject consultants have virtually disappeared. Without expertise and collaborative services, teachers are being asked to engage in the fight against bullying empty-handed. They need anti-bullying curriculum documents, lesson plans, and talk-therapy experts to guide them through whatever programs are implemented; they need qualified personnel to deal in depth with intransigent cases. Punishment is easy. If boards want anything more, they'll need to allocate funds to get it.

• *Supporting special programs*

Research has shown that students withdrawn for programming, such as special education or ESL, are two to three times more likely to be bullied. At the same time, budget cuts strike hardest at this kind of program. These programs need adequate funding not only to provide vulnerable students with essential survival and coping skills, but also to provide further support as students are reintegrated into the regular stream. Student bullies equate the lack of skills with weakness. Programs that allow students to develop those skills *are* anti-bullying programs.

• *Restructuring curriculum*

The only approaches to anti-bullying that have shown positive results are whole-school programs. That kind of commitment has to be structured into the school day or it won't happen. Add-ons get short shrift in a contemporary school's crowded day. If boards expect anti-bullying programs to be implemented at every grade level, and teachers and principals to adhere to the follow-up procedures and accountability measures that make these programs effective, space has to found in the curriculum. Where do these programs fit into the curriculum? What can be removed to make room for them? Unless these questions are answered, a commitment to anti-bullying is an empty promise.

• *Providing leadership*

If a school board makes a public commitment to implement anti-bullying guidelines, not only in every school for students and adults alike, but in every office in the board from the director of education on down, that one act would do more to eradicate bullying from schools than everything that has been done in that board up till now. Students bully, but so do adults. With the proper leadership, bullying could be stopped top-down as well as bottom-up.

Education: "Push-Me Pull-You"

In asking our schools to serve contradictory functions, we strain the credibility of our school environments and contribute to our inability to adequately deal with bullying.

Young people can be excused if they enter school trying to make sense of the world and wind up confused and conflicted. They look to schools for direction but, much like the Push-Me Pull-You, the two-headed llama in *Dr. Doolittle*, they have to survive in spite of always facing in two different directions at the same time.

Anti-bullying programs have to work. In a bullying school, everyone loses.

With school boards, principals and teachers, and parents pulling in the same direction, any school can be transformed into an anti-bullying school. And in an anti-bullying school, everybody wins.

In asking our schools to serve contradictory functions, we strain the credibility of our school environments and contribute to our inability to adequately deal with bullying. We trumpet our desire to educate students to the utmost of their individual capacities, for example, while we demand that schools sort and rate students with a battery of standardized tests. We want our schools to offer all students an equal chance to succeed, but we allot insufficient resources to support students with different emotional, social, physical, or intellectual needs. We want students to learn how to cooperate with one another and collaborate within a group for the benefit of all; meanwhile, we reward students within a highly competitive system predicated on individual excellence. We expect schools to inculcate in students the fundamental values of the society, but we try to accomplish this socialization within environments that are, to varying degrees, sexist, racist, homophobic, and elitist.

If students come to school confused or conflicted in any way about aggression, competition, and status, the mixed messages embedded in the environment can fuel misapprehension. When should students cooperate and when should they compete? How do students keep from losing when they do compete? What's wrong with putting people down, finding an edge to use to your advantage, or making a distinction between "us" and "them" when everybody does it, even the teachers? What's wrong with being aggressive? In the eyes of a student bully, aggression is rationalized as strength, competitiveness as licence to prey on others, and bigotry as a proof of status.

In the final analysis, bullying of all kinds left unattended eventually leads to a creeping cynicism and a loss of faith in the fundamental values on which society is built. When bullies thrive in the midst of anti-bullying sloganeering and half-hearted implementation, their presence only reaffirms for everyone else that might *is* right. Anti-bullying programs have to work. In a bullying school, everyone loses.

As this book has shown, however, bullying can be stopped. When everyone involved in a child's education begins pulling in the same direction, schools can be transformed. When school boards assume a leadership role in reaffirming everyone's right to be respected, anti-bullying is energized. When principals are as accountable to their teachers for their behavior as teachers are to them, anti-bullying is strengthened. When parents accept how crucial parenting styles are to inhibiting aggression in children, anti-bullying is vitalized. With school boards, principals and teachers, and parents pulling in the same direction, any school can be transformed into an anti-bullying school. And in an anti-bullying school, everybody wins.

Conclusion: An Old-fashioned Idea

We live in a competitive culture. As long as we teach our children the right way to compete, there's nothing wrong with competition. But competition becomes an aberration when we see only a dichotomy of winners and losers, celebrating the first and denigrating the latter. When competitors are unevenly matched and the outcome is predetermined, victory is hollow and defeat demoralizing. True competition is engaged between equals. Anything else is exploitation.

We need to teach children when not to compete. When an aggressive individual exploits a vulnerability and triumphs at someone else's expense, that's not competition; that's bullying. When it's time to make a decision, solve a problem, or maximize learning, children need to work together. When individuals of differing ability, backgrounds, and experiences collaborate, the power of the group is greater than any one person. Parents sometimes object to collaborative group work on the basis that the least capable students benefit from the work of the most capable. Research has shown otherwise. When one student tutors another, both benefit, but the tutor learns the most.

Respect for one another in schools liberates students to make prosocial choices: when choosing sides for a game, they're free to pick the worst athletes first, just to make them feel better; they can introduce themselves to a shy, introspective newcomer and sit with that person at lunch; they can offer to pair up with a struggling ESL student in class to guide the student through a difficult activity; they can recognize a bully's machinations and repel them.

The Golden Rule

It's no coincidence that at least a dozen world religions embrace the same value in the central core of their beliefs. Here are a few examples:

- Treat not others in ways that you yourself would find hurtful. (*Udana-Varga* 5.18)

- In everything, do to others as you would have them do to you; for this is the law and the prophets. (*Bible* Matthew 7:12)

- This is the sum of duty: do not do to others what would cause pain if done to you. (*Mahabharata* 5:1517)

- Not one of you truly believes until you wish for others what you wish for yourself. (*Hadith*)

- What is hateful to you, do not do to your neighbor. This is the whole Torah; all the rest is commentary. (*Talmud* Shabbat 31a)

People with and without faith recognize one principle as fundamental to a fair and just society — respect. It is the foundation of a child's insistence on fairness. All children can articulate the concept that it's not fair when one person isn't treated as well as another. But the words aren't enough. If we could display each day to others the respect we want our children to display, we would be teaching them more than the words. If parents and guardians, school administrators, principals, and teachers resolved to always respect the rights and feelings of children, children would learn to respect other children and, ultimately, themselves. If we could instill that kind of genuine respect in our children, a generation would grow into a world without bullies. It may be a simple, old-fashioned concept, but the most potent anti-bullying program we know is justly named The Golden Rule.

Glossary

The definitions in this selected glossary reflect the meanings that are used in the text.

achievement: the attainment of specific learning goals in a school setting
affective: a term from psychology referring to emotional activity.
aggression: subjugating someone through an unfair or irrational use of power
at risk: a descriptor applied to students with academic, emotional, or social difficulties, or a combination of these difficulties, serious enough to jeopardize acceptable progress in school

brainstorming: generating a list of examples, ideas, or questions to illustrate, expand on, or explore a central idea or topic
bully: someone who uses an imbalance of power to repeatedly aggress against and harm another through physical, emotional, or social means
bystander: someone who witnesses someone bully another

cognitive: a term from psychology referring to intellectual activity
collaboration: problem solving in pairs and in other small groups (see also *cooperative learning*)
conflict resolution: an in-school process using peer mediators to resolve conflicts between and among students
control disorders: clinical conditions suffered by students who are unable to consistently monitor and regulate their own behavior
cooperative learning: a variety of small-group instructional techniques focusing on peer collaboration
curriculum: at one time, a synonym for syllabus; the current definition, which reflects the complexity of learning, refers to everything that happens in a school
cyber bullying: using the communication capacities of computers to bully others

detention: a form of punishment in a school in which an individual is detained and confined in a specific location during the school day
diary (private): an in-class record of personal observations, random jottings, and thoughts and feelings; shared only if the student agrees
discipline: the practice of establishing correct order and behavior in a classroom using such methods as rules, direct instruction, and punishment
drama in education: involves all students in the classroom in spontaneous, unscripted, unrehearsed activities; no audience is present

ethnocultural: identifying with a group of people sharing a heritage ancestry as well as other characteristics which might include physical, cultural, linguistic, or religious components

evaluation: determining progress toward and attainment of specific goals; assessing student progress and achievement as well as program effectiveness

exceptionalities: physical, intellectual, social, and emotional characteristics that mark an individual as significantly different from the norm; the difference may signal either a gifted or deficient development

gay: a term generally accepted to refer to both male and female homosexuals, but which is often used to denote males alone

homophobia: an active hatred of, dislike of, or discomfort with people who are not heterosexual. Homophobia includes prejudice, discrimination, harassment, and acts of violence brought on by fear or hatred.

homosexuality: a sexual orientation in which a person feels physically sexually attracted to people of the same gender

instruction: the established plan of actions and content specifically chose to enable learning

lesbian: a contemporary term denoting female homosexuals

literacy: the ability to read and write; often extended today to include the processing of information from all sources and systems, including electronic and micro-electronic

literature: writing of high quality and significance because of a successful integration of such components as style, organization, language, and theme

media literacy: the ability to analyze and reflect on the ways in which media events are formulated and how they function

mentor: a trusted and accomplished person who takes a personal and direct interest in the development and education of another

modeling: the act of serving as an example of behavior: for example, when a teacher displays a genuine courtesy toward others and a respect for individual differences

posse: a slang term for hangers-on in a clique or gang; individuals who are subservient to the leader of a clique or gang

prosocial: a term from psychology that designates behavior that conforms to the generally accepted rules of social interaction and personal and property rights

Queen Bee: a term popularized in the book *Queen Bees and Wannabes* by Rosalind Wiseman to refer to the dominant leader of a female clique

read-alouds: any material read aloud, often by the teacher; can be fiction or nonfiction

relationship bullying: employing such methods as rumors, name-calling, cliques, and exclusion to bully

risk-taking: the internalized understanding that mistakes or approximations are good; the freedom to experiment, extend the known, or try something new without unduly worrying about failing or being wrong

role playing: exploring the thoughts and feelings of another by behaving and responding as that person

same-sex: a term coined to refer to a context in which one gender is involved, as in the phrase "same-sex marriage"

sexual harassment: sexual behavior that a reasonable person should have known was unwanted or likely to be unwanted and distressing

sexual orientation: a person's emotional, physical, and sexual attraction and the expression of that attraction; a characteristic probably set at birth

standardized test: a test with established norms to enable comparisons; for example, the Stanford-Binet Intelligence Scale

stereotyping: to hold a commonly held view, often simplified and rigid, of the characteristics of groups of people

student–student bullying: bullying in which both bully and target are students

target: the object of a bully's aggression

Tribes: a prepackaged program involving a year-long series of lessons designed to increase prosocial behaviors and teach cooperative learning skills

writing-in-role: extending the ability to grapple with problems and issues from a number of different perspectives by role playing in written form

zero tolerance: a formal policy in which a code of conduct is strictly enforced; all infractions, regardless of seriousness or justification, are punished

Selected Bibliography

Since the topic of bullying in schools is finally receiving the attention it deserves, the field is rich with any number of excellent texts, studies, and commentaries. As this book developed, the following references emerged as touchstones. The list is decidedly idiosyncratic, and notable for the many fine texts not mentioned.

Dellasega, Cheryl, and Charisse Nixon. *Girl Wars: Strategies that Will End Female Bullying.* New York: Fireside/Simon and Schuster, 2003.

Dishon, Dee, and Pat Wilson O'Leary. *Guidebook for Cooperative Learning: Techniques for Creating Effective Schools.* 3rd ed. Holmes Beach, FL: Learning Publications, 1998.

Futterman, Susan. *When You Work for a Bully.* Montvale, NJ: Croce Publishing Group, LLC, 2004.

Fried, SuEllen, and Paula Fried. *Bullies, Targets, and Witnesses.* New York: M. Evans and Company, 2003.

Geffner, Robert A. *Bullying Behavior: Current Issues, Research, and Interventions.* New York: The Haworth Press, 2001.

Heins, Kathleen M. "Bullied . . . by the Teacher?" *Better Homes and Gardens,* September, 2003.

Lind, J., and G. Maxwell. *Children's Experiences of Violence at School.* Wellington, NZ: Office of the Commissioner for Children, 1996.

Namie, Gary, and Ruth Namie. *The Bully At Work.* Naperville, IL: Sourcebooks, 2003.

Olweus, D. *Bullying at School: What we know and what we can do.* Oxford, U.K.: Blackwell, 1993.

Parsons, Les. *Response Journals Revisited.* Markham, ON: Pembroke Publishers, 2001.

Parsons, Les. *The Classroom Troubleshooter.* Markham, ON: Pembroke Publishers, 2003.

Randall, Peter. *Adult Bullying: Perpetrators and Victims.* New York: Brunner-Routledge, 2003.

Rigby, Ken. *Stop the Bullying: A Handbook for Schools.* Markham, ON: Pembroke Publishers, 2001.

Sullivan, Keith. *The Anti-Bullying Handbook.* New York: Oxford University Press, 2001.

Wiseman, Rosalind. *Queen Bees and Wannabes: Helping Your Daughter Survive Cliques, Gossip, Boyfriends, and Other Realties of Adolescence.* New York: Three Rivers Press, 2003.

Index